Watching *the* *Creek* Rise

by

Sandy Reid

Copyright © 2022 by Sandy Reid

All rights reserved. No part of this publication may be reproduced, distributed, or transmitted in any form or by any means, including photocopying, recording, or other electronic or mechanical methods, without the prior written permission of the publisher, except in the case of brief quotations embodied in critical reviews and certain other noncommercial uses permitted by copyright law.

ISBN-978-1-951300-45-6

Liberation's Publishing LLC
West Point - Mississippi

Watching *the* *Creek* Rise

Table of Content

The Creek Bed 1

Ebb and Flow 5

Ooh-rah! 7

Sisters 17

Gumdrops 21

Fruit of The Spirit 29

My Salvation 37

White Paper Bags and Candlelight 39

Lights of Memories 43

In The Stillness 47

The Man, The Mantle, The Miracles 53

Muddy Water 57

Empty Toilet Paper Rolls 87

Satan Loves A Slough 91

Taproots of Faith 97

He is Faithful 109

Which Lion Do You Follow? 119

When the Dam is Broken 123

Salt Water, Sun, Sand, and Reflections 129

Conclusion 137

Sandy Reid

Dedication

This book is dedicated in memory of my wonderful grandparents. I will forever appreciate the love and spiritual foundation they gave me. May I never forget my roots, and may I always keep the faith.

Chapter One
The Creek Bed
The Foundation or Bottom of the Creek

As a child, I heard my granny say, "Lord's willing and the creek don't rise" many, many times. This concept of a creek rising and prohibiting someone from doing what he/she had planned has been at the front of my mind for a while. At times I giggled inside as I remembered her voice's inflection when she said those words. Most recently, I sensed there was a lot more to that quote than I had ever realized. Time has been fleeting by and with each passing year, I have noticed the loss of many of our foundational principles. I felt compelled to write this book but thought of every excuse to keep the words to myself. I fought the voices of discouragement and determined silence to be the culprit of a lot of our lost traditions and slippery foundations. So, I decided to take the leap of faith and fervently write as I felt led. As you read, I pray for the words to pierce doubt and darkness and awaken your purpose, to stir the waters of your soul.

Everybody has a life story. The pages are blank on the day you are born, but everyone has a certain number of pages to fill. The "dedication segment" of our life book is to what cause or purpose we give ourselves. The chapters are what we live. It has become commonplace to hear the words of Vikas Malkani, "You are the author of your own life story." What we do with our pages and how we create our story is what makes us unique. Regardless, we learn from not only our book, but from the books of others. Thus, my story...

A creek bed is the foundation or channel of a body of water, usually a stream. Most creek beds are a combination of rocks, sand, or plants which serve as the layer of protection or a boundary. The purpose of the creek bed is to prevent erosion of the banks and to allow water to flow freely from one channel to another. The beauty we see is the pristine flowers and hedges, the smooth rocks, and the tranquil flow of the water. What we don't see is the long trench, the hard work to dig the trench, and the steadfastness of the items placed to go to war against anything sent to destroy the flow of the creek.

So why the lesson about a creek bed? I'm glad you wondered. As I mentioned before, our lives are built day by day. They are a collection of things and a process of work, struggle, and satisfaction. A person's foundation is essential to his/her stability, purpose, and vitality. Our childhood, our family, our circumstances and experiences collectively create our trench by which waters pass. As youngsters we are not really in control of our path, so the trench is carved out slowly and by multiple people and events. As we grow and begin to make our own decisions, we add layers around our trench, and, oftentimes, we change our path. We develop our "creek bed" and pile on sand, rocks, and vegetation along the way. The question is, how careful are we when we select the items to help guard our creek/self? Do we just add the things that look like the other creek beds because it seems to be working well for them? Do we think about the purpose? Do we know the area in which we are assigned? Do we determine the best defense for our homestead? Do we allow the instant fixes offered by discount stores and social media to line our path? Do we carefully guard our ground and protect it? Do we really understand the value of those layers and the purpose of our stability and longevity? Do we see the power our creator has given us to spread the good news to all areas - like water trickling from one channel to multiple bodies?

The bible teaches us to put on the full armor of God, to plant our feet on the rock. Creek beds-if created properly- provide the visual masterpiece of hundreds of different bodies of water meeting together without the sight of the ugly, deep trench. Without the foundation of the creek bed, the beauty doesn't exist. Without our childhood- the good and the bad, without our less than perfect decisions as adolescents and adults, our trench isn't developed and adapted for its overall purpose. Our faith isn't tested, tried, and confirmed. When trials come and life hits us hard, we can either guard ourselves and have faith, or we can respond as a creek bed that lacks a good foundation. If we choose the latter, we begin to erode, wear down, and become an unruly force with which to reckon.

Thankfully, we have a God who will gladly help us clean out our trenches, will help us plant ourselves around positive people and will provide a path of purpose for us. "He brought me up also out of an horrible pit, out of the miry clay, and set my feet upon a rock, and established my goings" (Psalm 40:2).

Sandy Reid

Chapter Two
Ebb and Flow

There is a tiny creek that runs from the noisy streets of Jacksonville, Florida, to the quaint neighborhood in which I grew up. The creek is directly adjacent to my childhood home. It has listened to my deepest secrets, provided hours of discovery, served as a backdrop for photos, and withstood the ever changing occupants on Amherst Street. There's something about a creek that makes one listen intently to the water as it trickles over the rocks and kisses the ferns and moss near the bank. A creek seems to have the ability to call out to the human soul and convince it to be still and reflect on life. The water tends to mesmerize and force stillness. Such was the case with the creek across the street from my childhood home.

The creek was long, and the culvert made it possible for cars to take travelers to and fro on the asphalt road. On the side of the road, a patch of dirt and grass formed a ledge that seemed to be glued to the worn brick wall. Both sides of the wall revealed moss between the mortar that held together the chalky red brick. Depending upon the circumstance that brought me to the creek, I would either sit with my feet dangling from the ledge, or I would walk down the worn path along the side of the creek bank. I found my first baby turtle in that creek. My sister lost a hamster (Boogie) in that creek. We spent hours splashing around and playing in that little oasis. Who knew that a small part of nature could have such an impact on a person?

Yet, here I am, nearly fifty years later, still thinking about the little creek with its jagged platform and serenity.

After several years of visiting the creek and playing within the perimeters of my mom's voice, I decided I was big enough to explore a little farther down the creek. Before I knew it, I had traveled about six blocks. I was so captivated by the beautiful scenery around me, I never looked behind me. I never thought about the possibility of snakes or hazardous materials. I was focused on what was ahead and explored the wonders within that little stream.

Years later, I have come to realize my life has been much like the ebb and flow of that little creek. I have experienced excitement as sensational as the waters that dance down the rocky aisle. I have set my focus ahead and met many great people and experienced wonders. Like the ebb and flow, I have also experienced devastation-like the stench-ridden litter that clogs the serenity of the calming waters of the creek. I have felt my life's flow stop suddenly and slowly re-route as decisions and consequences forged a new path. I've had days when people have looked on as I have accomplished something great; I have had days when people have trampled the path of my heart's desires and dreams.

To this day, that little creek still remains tucked away on Amherst Street. It has survived the elements and all the things to which life has exposed it. I, too, have survived. Does a creek experience ebb and flow? Indeed it does, as do the humans who find solace in its existence.

Chapter Three
Ooh-rah!

Everyone deserves a love story of his/her own. My parents were no different. My mom and dad met while my mom was in high school. My dad had a job at the local Burger King located approximately three miles from Mom's house. Dad was a handsome guy! He had dark hair and hazel eyes. His cheekbones and chin seemed to be chiseled to a perfect compromise of masculinity meets model. He was a hard worker, and everyone spoke about his kindness. Granny always said he was a true gentleman. He loved my mom, and he loved Jesus.

Figure 1 My Dad

He and Mom spent their honeymoon in Hawaii and their first child was born in California. Dad joined the United States Marine Corps and served in the Vietnam War. Cell phones and Social Media did not exist during that war, so Mom and dad communicated via letters and photos. Dad served his country well. He was very intelligent and was featured in a few pages of the hardbound books published by the Corps. After the long, grueling months spent at war, Dad came home. He made it back. From the previous few sentences, you may conclude that the love story was a bit too perfect; maybe you should keep reading.

As time went on, Mom and Dad purchased a three bedroom brick home on Amherst Street in Jacksonville, Florida. They were thrilled to begin their life together and expand their family. Almost out of nowhere Dad began experiencing symptoms. He had served in a war; he had been exposed to Agent Orange; he was a United States Marine. The horrible chemical used in warfare was now turning its gnarly teeth on my father's body. Numerous tests confirmed Dad had a type of cancer caused from Agent Orange exposure. It was the early 70's, so doctors were not at all confident, nor well educated on how to treat such a dreadful disease. The doctors did their best to help our Marine beat the odds stacked against him.

Figure 2 Dad at bootcamp

Dad underwent a surgery to have his arm amputated from the shoulder down. The doctors tried to assure my mom they had gotten all of the cancer. That's when the tenacity of a true fighter showed up. Dad had a long road to recovery, and he had a young daughter eager to enjoy the playful days most dads and daughters share.

The Veterans Hospital did the best they could. The rooms of that hospital were filled with hundreds of sick people. Sadly, Dad was one of many. Dad embraced his new life and continued to wear his shirts starched to perfection. He learned to do everything with one arm. Mom said he never complained about the loss of his arm or the diagnosis of cancer. His goal was to live a life of love and happiness with his family. He was thankful for each day he managed to do that. Soon, dad was notified about his next procedure, and he was fitted for a prosthetic arm. The prosthetics in the 70's were not even close to resembling a realistic member of the body like prosthetics do today. They were cold, hard steel. In fact, the "hand" was more of a claw. It had three prongs- like a small gardening tool. Regardless, Dad was once again proud to gain part of his life back.

His biggest hobby was racing Corvettes. He was a member of the Corvette Club on Cassat Avenue, and he could not wait to test his new prosthetic behind the wheel of his white Vette. He was feeling better, and he had complete credence that he had overcome cancer. Candy, my oldest sister, was proud of her daddy. She learned to climb in his lap and accept the cool feel of the "Captain Hook claw" when it graced her face or back. Together they celebrated Thanksgiving, Christmas, Easter and birthdays. Mom and dad seemed to steal life back and recaptured the dream they had begun the day Papa united them in Holy matrimony. Their little brick home was filled with friends, family, and laughter once again.

As spring arrived again, Mom announced she was expecting their second child. The excitement and anticipation of their newest addition was quickly subdued as Dad began to feel unlike himself again. As abruptly as the cancer seemed to dissipate, that same monster appeared again. This time, the cancer had spread throughout his body. It had attacked his bones, and it was making its way to his brain. How could this happen? What about his wife and children? An answer life harshly replies to all- cancer doesn't care, and tomorrow is not promised to anyone. Prayer warriors took their places on the front line, and Dad kept the faith. He had good days and bad days. He loved to talk to his family, and he often placed his hands on Mom's stomach and talked to his unborn child.

The swing of emotions Mom dealt with was relentless. Dad had been to war, but mom battled a war of her own. She had to hold on to faith and find the strength her husband had always shown her. Towards the end of the third trimester, Dad's health worsened. The heartless disease had spread to his brain and caused him to, at times, lash out or behave as a completely different person. Taking care of him was a daily struggle for a young, pregnant mother of a toddler. On the good days, Dad would talk to Mom and tell her he loved her and how he would make it to see his new baby girl. On the bad days, with pain surging through his body, he still managed to say he would fight to survive. His birthday was March 10th, and the new baby was due in January. He had just a few months to go.

Once again the cancer dealt a devastating blow. Dad was not responding to any of the medications and required more morphine to stop the pain. Morphine is the drug used in war. Morphine is both a blessing and a curse. It can get a child through the pain of a severe burn, but it can also ease the pain of a dying body. Most of my experience around the drug has led to the latter.

At seven months pregnant, Mom was becoming quite plump. Her dark, black wavy hair shined like the long string from a cassette tape. She kept it teased high and pinned back. Her green eyes and dark lashes didn't require her to wear much makeup, nor did she feel like wearing it. What her eyes didn't show was the anxiety and fear of what was to come. Her eyes didn't reveal the emptiness she was feeling as her heart ached for normalcy again.

The last few days of Dad's life were spent confined to a bed. Dad didn't make it to January. Mom finished the last two months of her pregnancy clinging to her three year old and carrying her unborn child. I was that child. I was born January 14, 1973. Just two months after the worst day of my mom's life, she gave birth to me. I'm not really sure what she felt. How could she feel? I wonder if I gave her enough joy to help heal the brokenness she carried? I can't imagine experiencing such a precious time while grieving. When I think about it, I fail to give my mom enough credit for what she did to give us a stable home life. She wasn't perfect, but she was tough. However she felt, it didn't change the way she nurtured us girls. We lived in the small brick house on Amherst Street, and we learned to be strong.

Maybe that's why I am seen by others as a strong female; although, sometimes that's not a good thing. I like to think it is the dynamic power and perseverance passed to me from both Mom and Dad. Such is true to some degree; however, my grandparents also added a deep-rooted grit. At times, the never give up attitude has served me well; other times, it has been a stubborn folly that leads to self-inflicted wounds.

It wasn't until I was a little older that I began to ask questions. Mom was always very honest with me, and my sister and I were always allowed to look through pictures Mom had kept for us. One day that stands out to me more than any other concerning my dad is the day my grandmother shared a very special tape with me. Remember, I disclosed to you that my dad was a fighter. He was determined to meet his new baby.

One Saturday I was at Granny and Papa's house and I asked a question about my dad. I was in the fifth grade, and Granny felt it was time to share a special treasure with me. She invited me to her bedroom and told me to sit patiently as she slowly opened the bottom drawer of her white-washed bedside table. She gingerly pulled out a box and a tape recorder. She said, "Baby, I am going to let you listen to something your daddy made for you before he died. I promised him I would play it for you when you were old enough to understand. He wanted me to tell you he loves you and will meet you one day in Heaven." My heart began to beat a little faster and my eyes widened as I realized Granny was unwrapping a cassette tape from the silky handkerchief she had placed in the box ten years prior. Out of all the time I had spent with Granny and Papa- literally every day I could- I never knew that gift from my dad was in my presence every single time.

"Now you will have to listen carefully because he was very, very weak. It took him a long time to get his words out, but he wanted you to know he didn't quit." I crossed my legs in a tight X and leaned forward without realizing how intent I was on listening. The recording was just as Granny said. It was slow. I listened as a twenty-five year old man wheezed and pushed hard to speak each word. I could picture his head and shoulders rising and falling as he spoke. Each inspiring, heartfelt word was spoken just for me. He told me he loved me. He told me to never give up. He promised to see me one day. The recording lasted for several minutes, mainly because of the pauses taken while he mustered the strength to speak. It didn't matter to me. I would have stayed on that bedroom floor for the rest of the day just to hear my dad speak to me. Finally, I felt like I met him. Those words-that moment- have never left me. In fact, I feel like those words were literally etched on the walls of my heart. The Ooh-rah spirit of my Marine still surges through me.

Like most people, I have been through many hard times in life. I have not always jumped back up and dusted myself off as quickly as I would have liked, but I have always kept going. I can't explain how or why other than it is like I have a "warrior spirit" rising from within me. I believe the Bible is God's living word, and scripture teaches us about passing blessings and behaviors from generation to generation. If the word is alive and can be spoken into existence, we have the power to keep going and to overcome. The bible teaches us in Proverbs chapter 18 verse 21, "Death and life are in the power of the tongue; and those to whom it is dear will have its fruit for their food." Jude 1:20 states, "But you, beloved, building yourselves up on your most holy faith, praying in the Holy Ghost...". The Word of God is alive, and because our Savior has given us the same power that allowed Him to defeat death, hell, and the grave, WE have power in our words! What we say (even to ourselves) is active. For that reason, I have to believe the warrior spirit my dad possessed was passed to me. Couple that blessing with the faith and strength I learned from my family, along with God's promise of the Holy Spirit.... and that is my how. I can't do it alone, and I may sink low, but my God is quick to rescue me. My favorite scripture is Matthew 28:20, "I am with you always, even to the end of the earth." It doesn't matter who leaves you or hurts you, God will always be with you. People disappoint, but God never fails.

The years that followed that special day when I listened to my dad's voice were filled with more questions and stories about my dad. I learned some very valuable truths: He loved Jesus. He believed in Heaven, and he was ready to meet his Savior. His favorite song was by songwriter Dottie Rambo- "Lord Build My Mansion (Next Door to Jesus)." He worked hard and believed in being clean and neat. My commitment from that special Saturday in 1983 was to one day meet the man who believed in love so much that he used his last few breaths to speak to me.

More importantly, my commitment is to meet my Savior who also gave his last breath just for me. Have you lost someone you love? Have you dealt with a parent who was never a part of your life? Have you wondered if you are enough? My friend, you are more than enough. In fact, when you were created God himself designed you. He wants to have a relationship with you- even though He has billions of others to love and communicate with- He wants you. He died for you. Don't let the words of negativity keep you down. Make that commitment to spend eternity with your Heavenly Father.

Sandy Reid

Chapter Four
Sisters

I consider my older sibling another gift I received. Hear me out. We have had our moments, but we have also shared a special bond. Candy and I grew up sharing many laughs and many tears together. We had a bond that my grandfather continuously nurtured. He reminded us that we should always "Stick together and take care of each other." We shared so many growing pains, and we have pulled each other from the emotional wrecks of life time and time again.

As adolescents, we enjoyed watching the newest music craze, MTv. On the days we missed school, we would pile up comforters on the sofa bed in the den. We would "vegg out" on junk food and puff a candy cigarette or two. I became her mannequin as she completed cosmetology school. She became my coach when I learned how to stick up for myself in school. We attended an elementary school just blocks from our house, but when it was time to go to junior high, we had to ride a bus to the other side of town. The other side of town meant the side with gangs, riots, and a lot of things we had never experienced before. We stuck together and learned to stand up for ourselves. I could probably write another book on the three different "levels" of schools we attended, so I will save those details for another day.

We were only four years apart in age. We shared some of the same clothes, the same phone (that actually stayed on the wall), and the same Christian values. We were by no means perfect, but we were a perfect team! We called ourselves the Howze sisters.

For some reason, I became extremely anxious and troubled at night. I would wake up in a complete panic and become physically sick for reasons nobody could understand. My home was safe, and I even had a cozy bed, but there was a spirit of fear that gripped me and tortured me. If you've ever had a nightmare, you can imagine the exhaustion of dealing with that each night. To top it off, I became a sleepwalker. I could escape a room or engage in a strange conversation while completely asleep. Candy became my security. Each night she would let me crawl into bed with her. She had a canopy bed draped with pink linens. It was like a princess bed to me, and it made me feel as if I had been freed from the darkness located in the very next room.

I would be blameworthy if I didn't take a moment to sidetrack and document the decor of a typical adolescent bedroom during the late 70's. As I noted already, the bed was a white, wooden design with a canopy of ruffles on top. The matching dresser held a large mirror, perfect for applying our blue eyeliner, tinted mascara, and strawberry flavored kissing potion lip gloss. On one side of the dresser, Candy kept her collection of perfumes- Loves Baby Soft, Anais Anai, and Gloria Vanderbilt to name a few. Her walls were white. The carpet was a trendy pink and white shag-like an inch long shag. She had a foot-shaped rug at the end of her bed. We would sit on or near that rug when we played boardgames or looked at yearbooks. The back of her wooden bedroom door served as a display for posters of her crush, Scott Baio and her hair envy, Farrah Fawcett. One of her black velvet marker posters of a panther in a garden also adorned her wall. She had a few black and white pictures of her modeling headshots, and the windows gave a view of the backyard and the neighbor's wall. Her sliding door closet was located on the left side of the room; it was full of "our" clothes and shoes. The walls held typical memorabilia, but most importantly, they held our Howze sister secrets. We shared all the details about our days, our friends, our dreams, and our problems. We learned to bury our faces in our pillows as we stayed up past bedtime giggling while creating silly song lyrics, dances, or other humorous moments. No matter what, we found a way to make each other laugh.

As we grew older, one of the most devastating days of my life was the day Candy moved into a place of her own. I literally felt like my heart would remain broken forever. My friends didn't really understand my sadness because they could not wait to get away from their siblings. For me, it was more than that. She really was my best friend. The separation anxiety was short lived as she and I were able to visit frequently and pick up right where we left off. She didn't forget about me like everyone said she would. We continued our shenanigans and learned to live apart without really losing each other.

Looking back, I can't imagine my childhood without her. We were a safe place for each other. We built a bond that we didn't fully understand until our age caught up to our experiences. Fast forward a few decades, several moves, deaths, births, and lives of our own-we still lift each other up. When I need a prayer warrior in my corner, I know who to call or text. When I hear a worship song or sermon that gives me chills, I share it with her as quickly as I can. We may not see each other as often as we should, but we are in contact with each other all the time. The sibling relationship Papa nurtured is one of the strongest, most beneficial relationships I have to this day.

Chapter Five
Gumdrops

Granny loved Christmas. She loved the cooking, the busy streets, the lights, the laughter, and the time with family. It is amusing to remember those times. I'm not sure how we all fit in that small, white house on West 18th Street, but we did- year after year. The large kitchen table was adorned with "pretties" as she would call them. Papa and I were always given the task of bringing in an extra table just for the desserts. We usually chose the octagon picnic table because it fit nicely in the corner of the dining room. Granny would drape a festive tablecloth on top before she arranged each delectable treat. I can still smell the pecan pies, and I can still see the homemade chocolate forming "spindles" as it thickened to the right consistency for frosting. The chocolate icing would dance across the seven tiny layers of cake Granny had cooled to perfection. That cake was my favorite, so she always had one ready for me. Another specialty sure to accompany the coconut cake and sweet potato pies was her simple jelly cake. It was a favorite among the older members of the family. Maybe it was because of the simplicity and goodness; maybe it was because it too brought back memories of their mother on Christmas day. My great-grandmother was a small framed, sweet woman who knew how to cook. Although it was just a homemade cake topped with apple jelly, a jelly cake was a treat to her family. Back then, indulgences like eating cake didn't happen often. Money was tight, and rarely did a family talk about having extra. One thing is certain though, the amount of love poured into the preparation of those special treats was carried on through my granny.

Everyone was welcome. The large, decoratively carved six panel pecan-colored door remained open on Christmas day. The glass door was cleaned and accessorized with jingle bells so everyone would know when another guest arrived. It's funny nobody cared about that tight little space in the living room. One by one, we made our way to the kitchen and filled our plates with delicious food. Cousins and friends found a place to sit around the floor of the living room. Our drink cups had to be nestled strategically between our feet and the thick, shag carpet. The senior adults were seated around the tables- Papa's sisters and brothers and some church family. The other adults were seated in extra chairs Granny had placed in both the dining room and living room. The teenagers and middle-aged group found a spot outside either on the porch or seated on the white iron lounge chairs under the enormous magnolia tree.

As we were eating, the traffic on the road was consistent. Most of the cars lined the road by Granny and Papa's house; the guests continued to arrive until late afternoon. I have tried and tried to think of a negative because today's world is so full of negativity and selfishness. I keep telling myself, surely everything wasn't as "magical" as I remember. But, I can still hear the sounds of Christmas music playing softly in the background. I still hear the very recognizable laughs from great aunts and uncles. I still hear the clanking of the dishes as Granny restocked the "buffet" line. What I can't remember hearing is negativity. Not one person complained about the seating. Not one person worried about not having enough to eat. Not one person argued or spoke harshly to another, not even Granny, who by today's standard would be justified for having a grouchy attitude.

Granny cooked everything except the Ham and potato salad (because those were my mom's specialties). Every single thing displayed on the stove top, along the kitchen counters and atop the extra table in the dining room was prepared by Granny. Granny didn't work and Papa had been injured at the Railroad years before I was born. He and Granny were called to ministry, and other than a few construction jobs, ministry is the only occupation I ever saw them carry out. Papa wasn't on a set salary. He believed he was called to minister to people and God would provide for them. I mention that because the lack of contribution by all of the guests would seem to provide another justification if Granny were upset about having to buy so many groceries to make our Christmas meal. She never did. She taught me about love and sacrifice. She explained to me year after year why cooking for everyone was so important. As I got older I realized what she meant.

I remember those hot, Florida Saturdays when Granny would tell me she was putting some of her money up for Christmas. Her little "nest egg" she called it. She would take five or ten dollars from her hand and fold it over and under to make a thin trifold. She would then slip the money in the groove under the left side of the kitchen cabinet. The special cabinet was located just above the spice rack. Month after month, she placed those neatly folded bills under the special cabinet. By December, she would count her "nest egg" and begin shopping the sales at the local markets. Fortunately, she and I were helpers and friends with the gardener neighbors, so we were able to gather pecans, greens, and fruit with them. Granny had a grapevine, a pear tree, a fig tree, and a pomegranate tree in her yard. We harvested those things to use as well. She never asked anyone to pitch in for our Christmas meal. Her attitude was not like the attitude most of us have today- if they don't bring; they don't eat. Her attitude was more of a belief that ministering to people was a full-time lifestyle, not a Sunday and Wednesday job. She believed having people gather around and sing songs, laugh, and share good food together also planted seeds of gratitude, humbleness, and kindness.

    Family was of the utmost importance. In Granny's mind, everyone was welcome to join our family. She was right. She taught me so many lessons and values that have taken years to grow to maturity. I am in no way what she was. I love to cook and entertain, but I have caught myself grumbling and stressing over things when that is not how I was taught. My heart has been bruised and sometimes hardened because of the winds and storms of life I have endured. As I mentioned before, people will disappoint you. Regardless of how I have messed up or how I have allowed people to upset me, I continue to feel the need to feed people and love them (and I still struggle with this sometimes). Those roots send surges of life to me. Just like Granny taught me: Family is important. Love and laughter are important. Christmas is magical. Motherhood is a high calling. God is faithful.

Some of the simple items Granny was adamant about using every Christmas seemed so pointless to me as a teen. For example, she insisted on displaying a plastic tree adorned with gumdrops. My oldest sister and I were always in charge of placing the gumdrops on the plastic gumdrop tree. Granny stored the tree in the original box and the gumdrops were one of her most pressing purchases two days before Christmas. I will admit, when we were younger, the gumdrop tree was fun to decorate. We would pour out the gumdrops on a plate and marvel at the extra sugar crystals that spilled out of the plastic package. The sugar crystals were like edible diamonds to us. We would work very hard to make sure we used every color only once, but at least once. I loved it when there were too many red ones because I would have to eat the extras to make sure nothing went to

Figure 3 Gumtree Centerpiece

waste! That bite of sweet cherry flavor combined with a crunch of light sugary "snow" lingered in the crevices of my molars for hours. I'm sure my dentist didn't appreciate the effect of gumdrop tree, but I sure did.

As teenagers, we were still in charge of the gumdrop tree. My sister and I would make conversational eyes at each other and laugh a little as we both knew we had the same question going through our minds. "Why are we still doing the gumdrop tree? Nobody eats the gumdrops. We will end up taking them all off and throwing them away this afternoon." Sometimes, when one of us felt really grown up and brave, we would ask, "Granny, are you sure you want us to do the gumdrop tree? I don't think anyone eats gumdrops." Without a hiccup she would reply enthusiastically, "Yes, honey! We have to have our little gumdrop tree. It's pretty. Somebody might want a gumdrop." And with that, we would begin to bite our smiles and place the gumdrops on the tree.

Interestingly enough, before we finished the tree, we would find ourselves sharing stories about the previous years we had spent decorating that little plastic tree. "Hey, do you remember that time….." Each gumdrop we placed on the tree came with a story. Thinking back, I can remember Granny standing at her avocado colored gas stove listening to us. After a few stories, she would chime in, "Girls y'all always stay close and spend time together." We would reply with the usual, "We will," but we had no idea how vital those conversations were.

As we became mothers ourselves, Candy and I made several

trips home for Christmas. Our children experienced the most important task of decorating Granny's gumdrop tree. We watched them pour the crystal-topped sweets from the package and sneak a gumdrop in their tiny mouths. They locked eyes and widened them at each other to signify the tasty goodness and satisfaction of their deed. As I watched them through the eyes of a mother, the unspoken lesson became clearer to me. The sibling memories were recounted and additional memories were made. There was innocent laughter and moments of love. It wasn't about the gumdrop tree at all. It was about quality time and togetherness. I'm almost fifty years old now. Granny has been gone for years. One of the first things my sister and I wanted to make sure we kept after she died was the silly little plastic gumdrop tree, the box still holding its fragile pieces.

Every December we talk about the significance of the gumdrop tree. Its significance is so resounding that I am compelled to make sure our grandchildren share the tradition. I have already figured out which store stocks the gumdrops so there will be no delay in carrying on this heartfelt tradition.

Of all the decorations, the lights, the bustle in town, the simple little gumdrop tree seems to have some of the deepest roots that hold our treasured memories together.

Sandy Reid

Chapter Six
Fruit of The Spirit

Christmas is a special time of the year. We get to celebrate the birth of our Savior and tell the story of His love for us. The concept of giving and showing others the love of Christ is not one of which I was deprived. Papa was the pastor of a small, country church in a town about an hour away from where we lived. We made that drive every Sunday and Wednesday without fail. Sometimes we had a smooth ride; other times, we had to overcome traffic, flat tires, and radiator issues, just to name a few. Regardless, the goal was to make it to church, and the efforts were relentless. In fact, Saturday nights were spent preparing for Sunday mornings. Granny wanted to ensure the morning would go smoothly, so she gladly accepted the responsibility of church day prep. I must admit, I cringed when I heard her say, "Sandy, it's time to get your bath and wash your hair so I can roll it for church tomorrow." See, I have naturally curly hair. I never felt the need to roll the already curly locks. Granny, on the other hand, absolutely loved Shirley Temple. Granny believed the curls could be trained to bounce as beautifully as little Shirley's. Thus, I endured what I considered agonizing hours of "roller do's."

Since I was a bit of a tomboy, my bathwater included a special ingredient that Granny felt most vital to the cleanliness of my filthy knees. While running the tepid bath water, Granny would add a cap full of Clorox bleach. If cleanliness was next to Godliness, I was going to be close! To add to the fragrant concoction, Granny would allow me to have one bath bead. The variety of colors always made the decision hard for me. The oil filled ball looked like a marble as it floated in the water. Gradually, the fragranced oil would melt away and attach itself to my body. Needless to say, my body must have smelled the most unique when I finished my bath. Granny kept busy picking out everyone's clothing for church. She and Papa always wore complementary colors. Papa's job was to surprise Granny by wearing off colored socks, which she would notice when he took the stage to play his guitar. I always wore a dress and some type of jewelry Granny let me borrow from her special jewelry box.

Figure 4 Papa and Me Working

Saturday night bath time was always scheduled around the start of one of our favorite TV shows, Hee Haw. Immediately following my bath, I would slip on one of Papa's big white T-shirts and take my place on the floor in front of the TV. Granny was in her seat behind me. She held in her hand one of my worst enemies- a comb. Remember, I had long, thick, curly hair. I would play all day with my hair the way I combed it, but it did not meet Granny's standards. I always liked to use Papa's blue brush with silver and black bristles. That brush smoothed the top portion of my hair perfectly, and I thought it did a great job of hiding the "rat's nest" of tangles near the nape of my neck. That hairstyle was fine for our Saturday yard work, but every Saturday night, that nest was disturbed.

Granny handed me the pink sponge rollers so I could unsnap them and hand them up one by one. I think it was to give me something to do while she rhythmically dismantled my nest. I usually cried and pleaded through the opening segment of our TV show. I thought every hair on my head was being plucked out one by one! Sometimes, Papa tried to come to my rescue, but Granny always won. She would go on to say she loved me and wanted me to look nice. She told me young ladies must always present themselves as clean and neat.

Figure 5 Granny and me visiting Six Gun Territory

Soon the show would be in full swing, and we would find ourselves laughing at the silly jokes acted out before us. By this time, my hair would be snuggled around the sponge rollers, ear high. I usually moved from my seat on the floor to Papa's lap. We sat in his big soft caramel colored chair. We would take turns singing with the stars of the show while picking our teeth with toothpicks. Papa loved his toothpicks, and I loved my papa. If he had a toothpick in his mouth, so did I. As the hours passed, we made our way to our rooms to sleep. I had the option of sleeping in any room in the house, but the only place I wanted to sleep was with my papa. I don't think I will ever be able to explain the security I felt when I was with him. He was like my angel. I had watched him overcome sickness and trials. I had seen him pray for people and lead them to Christ. I had witnessed the boldness with which he spoke the Word of God to others and over us. He had the most faith of any man I had ever been around. As I made my way to his room, I would glance at the picture on his bedroom door- the huge angel hovered over the young children as they crossed a bridge. She was their guardian angel, and I knew in my heart Papa was mine.

I can remember being sick as a young child. Every time I was sick, I wanted to go to Granny and Papa's house. I felt like I would be safe there. My thought was sickness could not stay; the devil was afraid of them because they were so Christlike. I knew without a doubt, when I made it to their house, the devil wouldn't be there. Every time I came, Granny set me up in the living room, and they prayed for me. My sickness went away every. single. time. Each time that occurred, my faith increased.

I remember one night in particular, I went to bed and Papa was called to the hospital to sit with a church member. Papa's bed was made of dark mahogany colored wood. The headboard and footboard had posts that, to me, resembled a chess pawn. As I tried to close my eyes and go to sleep, I felt a fear come over me. It was a familiar feeling, the one I had before when I would have to go to my sister's room to sleep. Papa wasn't in the room with me. It was dark. I peeped out of my right eye and noticed what looked like a strange silhouette. My fear began to gain control of me, and I felt as if I could hear the devil making fun of me. "Where is your papa now, little girl? I can make you sick if I want to." The bed began to look more like a scary shape, and my heartbeat picked up its hurried pace. All of the sudden, I looked at the door. I remembered the picture. I remembered the words I had been taught. "Speak the name of Jesus and the devil has to go." I started by saying it to myself, my eyes closed so tightly they made wrinkles across my nose. Slowly, I found myself gaining more boldness. I believed what I was saying. I sat up in that bed and looked directly at that strange shape. With my wrinkles across my nose now changing from fear to firmness of voice, I stated, "You can't stay here or hurt me because Jesus is in this room with me." I felt accomplished! I felt like I had done what Papa would have done. I had boldness and peace. I laid my head on the pillow and drifted off to sleep.

Throughout my life, I have had to rekindle that childlike faith. The older I have gotten, the harder it is at times. One would think such an experience would make it impossible to squelch faith. Yet, faith is something that has to be nurtured. Fear is one of the enemy's favorite weapons. He uses it to cause us to doubt and feel with our flesh rather than walk in the spirit. I have found myself speaking to the devil- out loud- numerous times in my life. "For God has not given us the spirit of fear, but of power, love, and a sound mind" (2

Timothy 1:7). Each time I battle with holy boldness, I am never let down. Jesus is still the sweetest, strongest name I know. I wish I could tell you I never doubt or worry because that's exactly what the bible teaches us, but I am still learning to give it all to God. I am still very human and yet very loved by God. He has never let me down, but I still have to remind myself to keep the faith. I'll discuss a little more in the next few chapters.

The church Papa pastored was tucked away on a road that quickly turned to dirt. The painted white church had a U shaped driveway just in front of the covered porch softened by the green outdoor carpet. A huge date tree was situated in the curve of the U and stretched out its fronds to leave a plentiful abundance of fruit each year. On either side of the U, a worn path was made by the constant rotation of tires across the grassy area. Both sides of the church were utilized for parking, both sides were paved only in the form of beaten down grass. Big paved parking lots and fancy buildings were not expected or needed. We didn't have a special facility just for the children and teens. We didn't have a balcony. What we did have was a group of people who had been touched by God. They had experienced a change in their lives that made them crave more. They had "tasted the goodness of our Lord." I am not saying a church with paved parking lots, balconies, or other buildings lacks such experiences. I am simply reflecting on what I experienced and how our expectation as a people was for God to move, and we believed he could do it no matter where we were. I can give thousands of examples of miracles and experiences in which I have had the pleasure to take part. I will do my best to recount many of them, but I do know my words still do not elucidate the true encounters.

Figure 6 Granny & Papa's house

Figure 7 Granny & Papa

Sandy Reid

Chapter Seven
My Salvation

I think it is only fitting that I begin with my own salvation. Afterall, if I am going to write about supernatural experiences, I think readers would want to know if I have ever experienced such encounters myself. To me, one of the sweetest memories I have is the memory of the confession of faith- my salvation. I was six years old. I had worn my light blue two-piece quarter zip polyester shirt and skirt. The shirt had Minnie Mouse embroidered on the right pocket area. I loved that skirt because it flared just a bit. Papa had preached a sermon that seemed to move everyone

Figure 8 The young Granny and Papa

in the building. As the service drew to an end, Papa asked everyone to make a large circle around the altar. We had done this many times before, but this night was different. As I walked to the front of the church, large tears began to fall from my eyes and slowly drip onto the red carpet. I was so moved inside; I could feel something deep in my chest.

We all made a large circle and held hands. Several people made their way to the center for prayer; some knelt at the altar. While my mom continued to play softly on the piano, I felt a tug on my heart to accept Jesus as my Savior. I walked to the altar and knelt down to pray. Soon, I felt my Granny's hand on my back. I shared with her that I wanted Jesus in my heart. Her tear filled eyes expressed a joy I will never forget. We walked toward Papa and I told him my desire. Together, they prayed with me and Jesus came into my heart. I was only six. I had not done anything major yet- no major sin...maybe a "white lie" here or there, but I was still in need of a Savior. At six years old I was given the gift of eternal life. It was a feeling of companionship embedded deep in my heart. I remember feeling like he really did move in!

My family believed in the Holy Ghost, laying hands on the sick, and God's supernatural power. As if my experience could not get any better, I was shown another part of His intimacy. As Papa laid his hand on my head and began to pray for me, I remember hearing the words, "The Lord says you are special, and you will do great things for Him. You are special in His sight." I felt a warm sensation cover my body, and the next thing I remember, I was waking up. I had been what Pentecostals call "slain in the spirit." Some people may think such a thing is a hoax or an act, but I felt it myself. I admit our world is filled with counterfeits and one must be aware, but for me, at six years old, there was no acting. That touch from God was true, real, and one I will never forget.

Chapter Eight
White Paper Bags and Candlelight

Another great memory from the little white church is the candlelight service we had each Christmas. Part of that service was also an outreach to our community. Weeks before the date of the service, we would pick up fresh fruit and white paper bags. We would form an assembly line and stuff each bag with a combination of apples and oranges. We would make sure the fold on each bag was creased and closed tightly. Finally, we would place the bags of fruit in the sanctuary. The next step was to make sure we had plenty of candles, matches, and tin foil. Over three decades ago, we didn't have the cardboard pieces or special cups to prevent the melted wax from attaching itself to our hands. We made a flower-like cover from aluminum foil. When grasped with the candle, the wax would slowly drip onto the foil and not on our hands. How simple….candles and fruit.

Year after year, the church would fill up with members of the community and with some faces we had not seen before. Time and time again, Papa would share the Christmas message of the love of Jesus. Each year the message touched the hearts of those inside the gray paneled walls of the church. The stories he told as we lit our candles and let our lights shine always seemed to have a new twist to them. Of course they did. That's the awesomeness of the Holy

Spirit- the all-knowing, softly tugging on the hearts of people to accept Jesus as their Savior year after year. Just like others have probably experienced, I must say, some of my earliest understanding about people came from events in the church. Christians are generally good people, but we are also human. Sometimes we allow our flesh/human nature to get the best of us (notice I used we). Such was the case of the man who decided he wouldn't come to the service if we couldn't guarantee him he would get a bag of fruit. While Papa wanted to give everyone a bag of fruit, he never verbally promised to do so. Of course we always had enough, and honestly, it really wasn't about the fruit.

In this specific year, the older man made his complaints known. I remember asking Papa why the elder would not come to church if he couldn't have a bag of fruit. At that point, Papa explained to me how God loves us so much and wants us to be his children. He wants us to love people even when they aren't easy to love. He also explained to me how the devil will use anything he can to try to stop salvation from happening. "He will even use a bag of fruit if he can keep a man from coming to church and having an encounter with God," Papa explained. Now, my demeanor is nowhere near as kind as my grandparent's, and I'm not always proud of the reactions I give to people. The thought of the man being angry and telling others he wouldn't come if he didn't know for sure he would get a bag of fruit made me think, "Guess you will miss out then." That's not the way Papa saw it. He used it as a springboard to smack the devil between the eyes and address the real issue. Again, it wasn't about the fruit from the trees. It was about the fruit of the spirit.

The Bible tells us "You will know them by their fruits" (Matthew 7:15-20). The Saturday before our service, Papa made a special trip to the man's house. He took with him one of the white bags of fruit. He also took me along. I remember Papa telling the man he didn't want him to be without the bag of fruit if it meant that much to him. He also told him he didn't mean to offend him or make him not want to come to church. The man was shocked and looked down as a tear slowly formed in his eye. His lip quivered just a bit and he said, "Brother Jones, you didn't offend me. I guess I'm just hardheaded and mean sometimes. I appreciate you bringing the bag of fruit." Papa seized the opportunity to meet the man where he was. He joked a little bit about age and grabbed his guitar to sing a few silly songs he had composed. A preacher singing songs about being old and broken doesn't fit the standard for an altar call; however, I watched that furrowed brow of the man gradually rise to his hairline. I heard laughter spring forth from his belly. Lastly, that afternoon, I heard him ask Jesus into his heart. Before we left, Papa played his guitar and sang a few Christian tunes with the man's wife chiming in on the chorus. The gentleness, meekness, humbleness, patience, and love tore away the walls of anger and helped open the man's heart to Jesus.

I never really thought much about being present that day. I was with Papa every chance I could get. However, I'm certain the seeds being planted that day were for me as well. People can be hard to deal with sometimes (including myself). Sometimes we just walk away and leave people alone because we don't understand their ways. Jesus didn't walk away, and he knew how sinful we would be. Jesus loved all of us so much he was willing to die on the cross for us. He expects us to show that same love and understanding to others. Wow! What a lesson a simple bag of fruit and the fruits of the spirit can teach.

Chapter Nine
Lights of Memories

Christmas memories are some of my favorites. I am sure this book will contain multiple accounts of Christmas related things, but I would be leaving out a significant portion of my childhood memories if I didn't include them...especially memories of Christmas lights! The city lights of Jacksonville were always something to behold, but at Christmas time, the city was turned into a magical light show. Each city street was adorned with lighted pole figurines, letters spelled out with greenery and tinsel, and each building was outlined in the brightest of colors. The store windows were dusted with canned snow, and the animated elves, gingerbread men, forest animals, and Santas moved to the rhythm of Christmas carols played softly in the background.

Every year Granny and Papa would organize a family trip to Jaimie Street. The homeowners in that neighborhood worked together to create an entire street of Christmas glamor. There was even a live Santa and Mrs. Claus! The manger scenes were life-size and adorned with twinkling lights and hay. Some of the neighbors served hot cocoa and cookies, and others greeted hundreds of families with smiles and small candy canes. The last time I visited that little Christmas village, one of the driveways had a huge, red mailbox where children could place their letters to Santa. Every detail was perfect. Every part of the magic of Christmas was captured. Although numerous cars lined the streets to park, there were no profanities being shouted in road rage. Everyone walked from house to house and spoke to each other in passing. Children held hands with their parents or guardians and walked swiftly so as to not miss one inch of lighted beauty. To a young child, everything seemed oversized and spectacular! The kindness onlookers exchanged and the excitement each setting brought with it, is something I will always remember.

Why can't the world operate like that all the time? Why do we get a surge of kindness and sentimentality during this season, but fight and rush through life the other eleven months of the year? There were no cell phones, no iPads, no pagers. The distractions we have now embraced as normal did not exist. Families simply spent time together appreciating the exquisite displays set before them. The homeowners may not have known what such a display meant to us, but to this day I do not believe I have ever seen such beauty nor experienced such Christmas joy exuded from kind strangers. Now, I create Christmas displays of my own. While they do not

Figure 9 My Mom and Uncle Sitting with Santa

compare to the neighborhood that inspired them, I enjoy watching cars slow down to catch a glimpse of Christmas magic.

Sandy Reid

Chapter Ten
In The Stillness

As the years have taken a "full speed ahead" approach, I find myself understanding the urgency of intercessory prayer. I value and cling to memories of old, wood-framed churches, dinners on the ground, and tattered, yellowed pages in hardbound hymnals. I hear the wise words Papa spoke about loving people and showing them the kindness of Christ. I replay sermons in my mind and realize how prophetic those spirit-filled messages were. I also find myself falling short time and time again. I miss having my spiritual mentors to lean on when I feel weak. Although this book has been filled with great memories and miracles, I must also include the harsh realities of sadness, anger, bitterness, and sin. I am not perfect. My family is not perfect. The older I get the more I realize how important it is that I remember my roots and draw strength from my Savior.

Just as a creek can rise, it can also run dry. I never thought I would have to say goodbye to Papa. Isn't that what we all think about someone special? I thought he would live forever and I would always have him to keep me strong. I realize I may have placed him on such a pedestal, which is probably not healthy, but I promise I have never met a man so grounded in his faith; a man so kind and loving. I was newly married with a beautiful baby girl when Papa began to suffer physically. I was 520 miles away, and we visited as much as possible. My last visit with Papa was one I will never forget.

My husband, new baby, sister, brother-in-law, and niece settled in our vehicles to make the long drive to Jacksonville. Each mile marker secretly tallied the last time I would cross that threshold to see both grandparents.

Figure 10 Grandpa and Kirsten

Papa's hair was still thick and white. His frame was thin, but his hands were still large, cracked, and firm. His blue eyes still had the little diamond in them caused by glaucoma surgery. But his smile... his smile was still infectious. He spent time holding Kirsten and playing with her. I'm positive he prayed over her too. My niece was also with us, so she spent time curled up in Papa's lap too. They played silly games and sang songs. He was frail, but still genuinely loving. The visit was short, but so important and so moving. I indulged in Krispy Kreme donuts and paid attention to every story recounted. As odd as it may seem, Papa knew his time with us was coming to an end. He knew this would be the last time he would see us. For the week we were there, I soaked up every sacred moment. He knew. I didn't. Afterall, since we had been there he had eaten more than he had in months. He actually sat in his chair at the dinner table and had guests come visit. He even managed to let the kids play horsey on his legs! In my mind, there were no signs of digression. Moreover, in my mind, Papa was invincible.

On the final morning of our visit, we unhurriedly began to pack up and prepare for the eight-hour drive to Mississippi. Papa continued to laugh and joke with us- as he was known for doing. If he felt heartache, he never let on. I could also tell Granny had enjoyed the visit and the jolt of vibrance it had given Papa. Through her smile, I could also tell she hated to see us go. She always did. Her reddening nose was invariably a dead giveaway to her sad emotions. As we said our goodbyes, one moment was very distinctly etched in my mind. Papa had already said his goodbyes, but I noticed he retreated to the back of the house and came back out again. As he called me to him, I noticed his face presented a different countenance than the one he wore only a few minutes before. He hugged me tightly for several seconds and kissed me. He pulled his arms back and within his large, warm hands he allowed my head to rest. He stared directly into my eyes and captivated my attention as he told me he loved me and he wanted me to remember something for as long as I live. At that moment, time seemed to slow down. My mind didn't understand what the odd vibe was, but at the same time, my heart was in tune with his. He began singing,

> "These things that I have and hold dear to my heart, they're just borrowed, they're not mine at all. Jesus only let me use them to brighten up my day, so remind me, remind me dear lord. Roll back the curtains of memories now and then. Show me where you've brought me from and where I could have been. Remember I'm human, and humans forget. So remind me. Remind me dear lord."

I was overcome with emotion, but knew exactly what he was telling me. I had heard him sing that song hundreds of times, but this time it was meant especially for me. The ride back to Mississippi was even longer than before. I remember feeling the urge to tell my husband to take me back and let me stay. That wasn't what I was supposed to do though, and as much as I struggled to accept it, I knew I had to go with my family. Days went by, and then two weeks passed. Papa was scheduled for colon cancer surgery and the doctors confirmed all of the details. He made it through surgery and Granny called as often as she could. The news was not promising and pricked the bitter thorn inside of me. He was such a servant for God. Surely he had more work to do! I prayed each day for him. I have to confess, part of my prayer was so selfish. I just wanted him here-on earth- with us.

Thinking back, I shamefully admit it was more about my feelings of uncertainty without him, and the importance I placed on my own child being around such a great man, my hero. I struggled with the conflicting reality that Papa was not well, and even though he was ready to see Jesus, I was not ready to let go. A few days later, I was cooking beef stew on the small white electric stove in our two bedroom trailer. I had Pastor Rod Parsley's church service playing faintly on the television while Kirsten was taking a nap. If I had it calculated correctly, Chris should have been on his way home from work. We did not have cell phones in the early nineties, so people never really knew someone else's exact location. We just used the approximate time frame from the end of the work day and estimated the time of arrival. I was stirring the dark, robust liquid surrounding the softening potatoes and carrots, and I had just added a little salt and pepper when I felt an urgency to read 2 Kings chapter 2.

I can't explain the yearning other than it was an extremely innate feeling that made me stop stirring the thickening gravy and stand still. I turned the oven dial clockwise to simmer and walked to my couch. I wasn't sure what the scripture was about. I couldn't recall anything about that particular book and chapter. As soon as I opened the bible and began to read, I couldn't make my eyes scan across the weightless paper fast enough- The story of Elijah and Elisha. How appropriate, yet how humbling and prophetic! The beautiful story of a mentor and his pupil. The adoration and respect was so evident. The story seemed to unfold a similar admiration and relationship I shared with Papa. As I said previously, he was my spiritual mentor, my father-figure, my hero. Tears filled my eyes as I felt a quickening in the depths of my soul. Somehow I knew Papa had crossed over the Jordan and the Lord was preparing me for what was to come. I sobbed and told the Lord I would accept a double-portion of Papa's anointing if that's what He was offering. Less than a half hour passed when my phone rang. Papa had shared the last few moments of his life telling Granny he loved her before he smiled, fixed his eyes toward Heaven and left this world behind. Although the message I had experienced earlier was truly special and one I still cherish, the pain I felt in my heart was overwhelming. How does a hero die? How will I get answers to the questions I may have about life or spiritual things? How do I carry such a mantle? I'm not even a great person. And lastly, how was I so fortunate to have spent time with such a kind and faithful servant?

Chapter Eleven
The Man, The Mantle, The Miracles

I understand I'm not the only girl who has ever had a wonderful grandfather. I know my story about Papa's love, service, and faith is one of millions in the world, but it is one I feel I must keep alive. If for no other reason, I must constantly remind myself of the tremendous responsibility and tasks at hand.

One thing is for certain though, I have not always exemplified the mantle or my Savior as I should. I am human and definitely have my share of shortcomings. Honestly, that is no excuse. I am in control of my thoughts and actions, so I should be able to do as I am called. Yet, I find myself falling short, and, at times, completely blowing the assignment. It is a constant battle, but isn't that also the spiritual warfare fought by Moses, Peter, and Mary? If I am being transparent, I deal with the same things many others also fight. Why me? Am I really capable? I mess up, so how can I do this? Who am I to say these things to others? Did I really hear from God or was that a moment of emotion? Can or should a woman even do this?

The fact is, being a Child of God is always a calling. WE are called to do great things, and we are reminded we, "Can do all things through Christ who gives us strength" (Philippians 4:13). That verse is given to us because He knew we would toil with the flesh vs the supernatural. He has not called us because we have it all together and never mess up. He has called us because He created us for a purpose. Let me repeat that (partly for myself). He created us for a purpose. He was not bored or trying to meet a certain number of "projects" for a quota. He created each of us with a plan already in place, a calling already developed. Our job is to submit to His will and direction and do as He leads. He has equipped us with His spirit and favor, but we must take the initiative to "Put on the whole armor of God" (Ephesians 6:11-18). That very scripture tells us the enemy will hit us with his wiles to corrupt our thoughts, tamper with our faith, and destroy our mission...IF he can. We must not be fearful! Our God has given us the armor to withstand such attacks. He only requires us to put it on. Therein lies the issue. We have to do something other than make excuses or put off what we know we are expected to do or say.

Again, I am guilty. I have been writing this book on and off for several years. At times I confidently typed as fast as the words were flowing to me. Other times, the words began to flow and I would continue tucking them away in a compartment of my brain as I told myself, "You can write it down later. Do you really think you have material someone else would want to read? People don't know you well enough to care about this stuff. Besides, you are going to make yourself look like some kind of fanatic or prodigal prodigy." I finally realized maybe this process was not just for the readers. This process was/is about my faith, my failures, my experiences, my testimony, my life, my mission. Most importantly, this is about making myself vulnerable and allowing God to do with me and or this text as He sees fit. It's about obedience.

As I compose each chapter, I am compelled to remember some of the sweetest moments in my life along with some of the most devastating. It has forced me to seek the Lord as Papa instructed, "Remind me. Remind me, dear Lord." If I lose sight of the memories that shaped me, of the mission before me...I lose sight of the Mantle and the Majesty of my Lord. No matter how tough the times have been or will be, I have to keep, "Pressing toward the mark for the prize of the high calling of God in Christ Jesus" (Philippians 3:14). I must finish the race. Too often, the discontent and negativity of this world zaps my energy and gives a false sense of doom. I have to keep typing the words. I have to keep believing in the purpose. I have to keep fighting the good fight.

I do believe there is a bigger plan for each of us. I believe the Lord will gladly open doors for us to meet new people and help change their lives for the better- if we trust Him and obey when he urges us to do things. A simple note, a text, a prayer, or even a shared confession can be the difference between someone throwing in the towel and someone hanging on to the promises of the Almighty God. Our human side would have us think such random acts are frivolous and counterproductive. But we are asked in the book of Isaiah, "Whose report will you believe?" Another verb God has shared with us. We have to take action. We have to believe; we must do whatever our "it" is.

You may be wondering what all of this means and why I wrote it or why you are reading it. Well, I can boldly say that I have been a part of many wonderful supernatural experiences and miracles. None of those things were because of me; however, I am so thankful to have those seeds of faith planted inside of me to help me grow. Throughout the book I mention various encounters and experiences. I hope they bless you and give you a desire to grow in faith alongside me. I'm not Elisha, but I am a broken vessel ready to accept a mantle and serve however the Lord sees fit. It's time for our generation to step up and heed our calling.

Chapter Twelve
Muddy Water

I told you I would be transparent. Thus, I must include some other defining moments that resemble muddy water more so than gently flowing creeks and harmonious family life. One of the things I have realized is no matter how great life is, no matter how dramatic and terrific childhood memories are, as you grow up you also endure pain, heartbreak, and devastating loss. Pain is an unwelcome guest, yet it squirms its way into our lives and takes many different forms. Sometimes pain is self-inflicted and sometimes it is devised by Satan himself. Either way, pain is not something I enjoy or seek. Oddly enough, I have often been the recipient of the self-inflicted type more than I care to admit. While I haven't physically assaulted myself, and I do not make light of those who suffer from such behaviors, I have a crazy way of either shutting people out or opening up too much.

When I love, I base it on the great love with which I was enveloped as a child. When I trust, I trust as if all people are still good and would never intentionally hurt or manipulate someone else. Boy, does that set me up for the trifecta of emotions I first mentioned- pain, heartbreak, loss! Thus, the water becomes a bit muddy. I know the right way to behave yet struggle to respond that way consistently. How can I love and give of myself if I am gambling with my emotions? How can I continue to give Christ-like compassion when I would rather retreat and wallow in solitude or anger? Why should I do any of these things if in the end I may find myself sitting in my favorite seat on my deck reflecting, wiping tears as they sporadically drop from my eyes, and warring with the fleshly monster that softly whispers, "Don't do that to yourself again. Just leave people alone." Afterall, who needs people, right? We do. We all do. In a murky mirage of regrets and relentless verbiage, lies the pinnacle of what we need- each other.

Proverbs 27:17 teaches us, "Iron sharpens iron." We challenge each other, hurt each other, pray for each other, hurt each other some more, love each other, and ultimately, we sharpen each other. I know, it's not what we want to hear when we are dancing at our own pity party. Although I haven't perfected anything- let's make that clear-I have started asking myself what I'm doing when I'm pulling away. Which model am I following, and what is the end result? Once again, the water churns and while the clarity emerges, the sedimentary gunk I've allowed to settle deep in my heart kicks up just enough muck to distort the clarity. I consider this process much like that of the disciples who ate, traveled, and witnessed with Jesus. They literally saw miracles and knew Jesus was a good man. Yet, when the pressures of the mob and naysayers increased, the disciples often missed the mission. They would whine and wonder why things weren't happening as they thought they should. Sometimes they had strong faith, and sometimes they seemed to forget everything they had learned. In the book of Matthew we read about how the disciples quickly boarded a boat with the intention of following Jesus. Jesus had just performed numerous miracles, and there was no indication of trouble. As Jesus took a nap, a storm began to push the waves against the boat. The winds became strong and unruly. Suddenly, the disciples looked at the circumstances and allowed fear to grip their hearts. They didn't speak boldly or even encourage one another in faith. Instead, they cried out to Jesus to save them. Jesus said, " 'Why are ye fearful, O ye of little faith?' Then he arose, and rebuked the winds and the sea; and there was a great calm. In other words, if Jesus is with us, we should not fear. We should encourage and remind each other that we are in the boat (life) with Jesus. To put it in modern terms, we shouldn't allow circumstances or social media garbage to create storms of fear, doubt, discouragement, or destruction in our life. We are on this journey together, so it is our duty to help one another stay focused, stay faithful, and stay fervent.

Heartbreak is the second emotion I listed. Heartbreak is so tricky because we must open our hearts to people and situations if we want to enjoy the rush of endorphins and exuberance of joy in which happiness can bring us. On the other hand, to open our hearts is like truly opening our flesh and making it susceptible to wounds, bruises and infection. How quickly we can go from awe-struck excitement to agony! Yet, to feel the rhythmic heartbeat with another, to know love and to be loved, we must throw our hearts on the table and risk heartbreak. Consequently, each of us must determine how often we are willing to take the risk. To me, heartbreak has often come in the form of disappointment, mostly from people who say they love me and never put forth the effort to show me. People who have spent hours, days, holidays, vacations with me and chose to slowly separate themselves, pulling away gradually as if their occasional absence would make the pricking of loneliness seem less detrimental to my heart. The words, "We will see" and "We should get together sometime" are often the culprit of such disappointment. Both phrases are the human way of letting someone down easy while making ourselves feel less offensive, less abrasive, less truthful. Both phrases are futuristic approaches that offer hope for fellowship and better days ahead. Similarly, both phrases let one "off the hook" without having to admit he/she has no true intention of following through. We make time for the things and people we value. If these two phrases are used repeatedly to someone, the phrases become the sum of that person's value- not presently important. What a concept!

A perfect example of my point is the large, loving family I mentioned in the first few chapters. The elders of the group were simple people. They grew up in harder times and knew the value of family. They did their very best to instill those values into the lives of their children and grandchildren. Unfortunately, life and "modern ways of thinking" also cast a vote and eventually vetoed the understood family bill. After Papa passed away, the family gatherings became less frequent and fewer were in attendance. At first I didn't think much about it because we all have busy lives and most of my cousins had grown up, had married, had moved away and had started families of their own. Over a decade later, I see the result of our busy lives; I rarely see anyone other than my own children and spouse.

Holidays are still very important to me, and I make sure I prepare everyone's favorites. Yet, there are no crowds of people anymore, no streets lined with cars. There are no groups of children running about with chocolate icing residue on their faces. There are no large family gatherings being held. The significance of spending time with the family that we cherished as children has now dissipated with little to no hope of returning. My children do not know most of their cousins. How can that be? I have one uncle living; I see him occasionally. How sad is it that we allow the very life we live to serve as an obstacle to the love of a family? I guess that is why I am so protective of my "little family." I try to create memories, take pictures, and build a relationship my children will cherish and protect as well. I am not perfect, but I understand the importance of family ties. Just typing this pulls at my heart and makes me feel so disappointed that our society has embraced more work and complex technology, but we have neglected our very own kin. We are guilty of stalking people online so we know more about their lives, but we ignore calls, texts, and visits from our own family members. It is a tactic of the enemy. What else have we let die with the generations before us? We must work fervently to keep our families close and cover them in prayer.

Lastly, I mentioned loss. Sometimes loss is in the form of a person. Sometimes the loss is in the form of yourself. Sometimes the loss is in the form of your confidence or relationships. Unfortunately, I have become well-versed in most of these areas. I can't apologize for elaborating even more about the loss of a person. If it seems overdone to you, please understand true love can never be overdone, and I have felt the anguish and emptiness that comes with grief more times than I would like to remember. However, each loss has taught me several things, and each loss has served as a point of maturity.

As I have already shared with you, when I lost Papa I felt like I lost my guardian, my hero, my Elijah if you will. Ironically enough, in the midst of the darkest time for me, God revealed so much truth. He taught me to be strong, and he impressed upon my heart the need to be bold and secure in my faith. As we made the trip back to Jacksonville, I held tightly to the memories and cried fresh tears each time I thought of what Kirsten wouldn't get to know. I was so disappointed that she wouldn't get to sing the silly songs while sitting on his lap; she wouldn't get to learn about music and meet the "music family" around whom I had grown up. She wouldn't have the security to crawl in his lap and hear him pray over her. She wouldn't see the miracles as God worked through him. I stared out the car window and watched the trees blur as we passed. What a loss. What a great responsibility Papa assumed, and what a sobering thought that now my husband and I were left to carry out that sacred duty. I was reminded of the song Papa sang, and yet it was so hard to imagine walking in that white-frame house and not seeing his smile or feeling the warmth of his large, rough hands. Who was I to even begin to fill such shoes? Yes, I did agree to take on the mantle, but the reality of moving forward seemed so unclear. I was twenty-two. I had a baby. I was a wife. I was also a very heartbroken granddaughter. I had to draw strength and do as I had been taught. I had to rely on the Holy Spirit to comfort and guide me.

We made the turn on West 18th Street, and I noticed the gate was already open. Granny was waiting for us to arrive. Nothing in the neighborhood looked any different from the few weeks before, but everything in my being felt different. I swallowed as firmly as I could and widened my eyes to see if the air around me would help dry up my tears. I had to face Granny. If I felt so torn apart, I could not imagine what she was feeling. The two of them had literally grown up together and tackled life's biggest storms together. What would she do without her soulmate? How would she ever feel whole again? Some people may think my level of perception and love for my grandparents are far-fetched and idol-like, but I choose to think of it as a precious gift.

When we entered the house, the smell was still the same. The wafts of fragrance came from carnival glass bowls filled with peach potpourri mixed with fresh fruit from the beautiful glass fruit bowl situated just so on the dining table. My eyes moved from right to left and the scenery seemed untouched. I quickly glanced to my left in the direction the carpet paved for the bedrooms. He wouldn't be walking down that little hallway. I wouldn't hear his throat being cleared as he stepped on the creaky floor. I shook the thoughts that tried to cloud my direction. I made my way to the kitchen. Normally, Granny would have met us at the door with her arms wide open. I knew she and I were both participating in the same emotional standoff. It would become real when we had to talk about it together. She knew how much Papa meant to me, and I thrived on the love the two of them shared. She looked up as I stepped in the dining room and faced the kitchen. Her arms opened in slow motion and her nose began to turn rosy. "Hey baby, it's going to be ok. He sure loved y'all." She mustered the strength to try to make us feel better when she was completely broken. She was truly a Proverbs 31 woman. "She [was] clothed in strength and dignity, and she [laughed] without fear of the future." One entire piece of her identity was gone. Life as she had known it had taken a complete turn. For the first time in my life, she broke down in my arms and we held each other tightly. We both understood the magnitude of grief we had to endure. We also understood we would see him again one day. One thing Papa always told my sister and me was, "If I go to Heaven before she does, you girls take care of your Granny." Instantly, those words echoed in my mind. As I looked across the room, I whispered to myself, "Yes, sir."

I must admit, Granny was a strong lady. She handled the funeral arrangements and all the visitors just as she always handled things- with class. The viewing was a representation of the impact Papa had on the lives of others. The lines were wrapped around the large funeral home inside and outside along the parking lot. Vehicles were parked so far down the road, police took their places to help direct traffic. Hour after hour, people stopped and shared a snapshot of how special Papa was to them. Story after story recounted the love he had for people and for his Savior. He truly was a man of God.

The day we laid him to rest, he lay in the blanketed surround - holding his thin, worn, black bible. Granny placed a picture of the two of them from their last wedding anniversary close to his head. He wore a wine colored suit- it was our favorite suit on him. His black cowboy style tie complimented the clothing.

As family and friends gathered on the day of the funeral, and the ceremony began, I couldn't help but sit in awe as I noticed the Lord had used this moment just as He refers to it in scripture. "Precious in the sight of the Lord is the death of His Saints" (Psalm 116:15). The sorrow I felt was unexplainably lifted as I witnessed people lifting their hands to Praise our Lord and bid a fine Homecoming to their dear friend and family member. It really was true. The Bible tells us the Holy Spirit is a comforter. Granny's head was tilted toward Heaven, and her hand was raised high. She worshiped her King in the worst of times. In return, she was given comfort and the peace of mind that she would one day meet Jesus and see Papa again.

I struggled to keep my nose from completely sealing off all of my airflow, and the tears continued to stream down my cheeks like tepid drips of water from a leaky faucet. I felt the loving touch of my husband's hand around my neck. He knew how hard this was for me, but he was so sensitive to my needs. Kirsten was just a baby, but even her behavior seemed to be reverent during this time.

The last thing I did was lean over to kiss Papa goodbye for one last time. Just thinking about it now, I can't keep a dry eye. Yet again, the Lord spoke to my heart. I gently leaned down and placed my head close to Papa's. I felt my tears move in reverse and stream through the top of my hair. I whispered, " I love you Papa. I need you. I need you." Unanticipatedly, I heard the still small voice reassure me I had to do this on my own. I had been trained, but I had to have a relationship with God all by myself. As I walked through the threshold of the exit, I vowed to do just that. I have been far from blameless on my quest, but I have clung to the teachings my papa gave me.

Over a decade later, I found myself in the agonizing grip of sorrow yet again. This time, I was a mature forty-three year old with two older children. During the course of at least ten holiday seasons and summer breaks, the children and I had managed to visit Granny and bring her to stay with us for a month at a time. She was referred to as "Little Granny" by my kids. They thought she hung the moon, and to her they were nothing short of sweet little angels. I had noticed Granny repeating herself and forgetting things as we spoke on the phone. When she came to visit, I could see her aged body becoming frail, and I listened to her recount the same stories time and time again. I never had the heart to stop her or let her know she had already told me that story less than an hour before. I was glad to listen and proud to have her with me. I prayed for her constantly. She and I had a connection that I still can't describe. She was a true prayer warrior. I've seen her kneel in her living room for hours at a time calling out to the Lord and praying for her loved ones. There is no doubt, she cultivated intercessory prayer in my life. Like most things, especially spiritual in nature, I soaked it all up but didn't practice it as often or as correctly as I should. Consequently, the peaks and valleys I've gone through have forced me to dig deeply and do what I know is right. Granny was never ashamed of her faith. She knew what she knew and nobody could take that from her. As gentle and kind as she was, she was something to reckon with if she had a mission of prayer! She didn't mind telling the truth even if it stepped on your toes. She did it because she loved her family. She loved us so much she wanted nothing more than to make sure we all knew Jesus and would be together in Heaven one day.

One Autumn, Granny came to visit again. At the time I had a small boutique, and my uncle stopped by so Granny could see me before I closed the shop for the day. I watched in disbelief as she gingerly made her way up the small set of stairs. Her clothes were not as tailored as they'd always been. Her hair was combed, but not styled to its usual perfection. Her wrinkled hands were trembling, and her lips lacked pigment. I took a deep breath and swallowed. I thought to myself, "Oh, my gosh! She has changed so much. I don't even know what to say." Her little round, blue eyes widened as she looked at the clothes and jewelry placed around the shop. Although she tried to pretend she knew what was going on, I could tell she was completely confused. I stepped up to her and hugged her. As if someone had flipped the switch on an outlet, she recognized me and embraced me with a hug and kiss. I explained to her what we had done to the old house I used as a boutique and indulged her in a story about the history of the place. When she left, I could barely focus on closing out the register as I kept telling myself she would be ok.

Truthfully, I was shook.

As was the custom, I pampered her like she had done for me all the years before. It was my honor and my duty to take care of her. She loved to be clean and neat. Remember, her famous quote was, "Cleanliness is next to Godliness." She loved jewelry, purses, and shoes. She liked to have her fingernails and toenails manicured and polished, and she loved the sweet smell of perfume. Her life had not been one of luxury, yet she always managed to put together a nice look. She believed in making her appearance represent her character.

One evening, I sat beside her on the couch and told her I would run her shower water for her and warm up the bathroom with the heater so she wouldn't freeze while bathing. She thanked me and watched me walk towards the master bedroom. It never crossed my mind that she may not remember what I said or where she was. If she weren't such an independent person, she probably would have sat there waiting for me to return for her. She didn't though. She walked to my kitchen and then turned to make her way back to the couch in the family room. She had also become confused about her surroundings.

My family room was an addition to the older model home Chris and I purchased two years after we were married. Originally, the family room was a carport with a door leading to the kitchen. When we remodeled, we closed in the carport and created a large family room with a small ceramic tile step that leads into the dining room and kitchen. It was at that spot of transition that my life took a sudden turn.

Before I could test the temperature of the water one more time with the back of my hand, I heard Granny cry out. Chris came quickly to tell me she had fallen down the step. My heart literally sank in my chest and rose again with a harder, quicker tempo. I ran to the family room and began to talk to her. Her cry of pain rendered me useless and guilty. How could I have known, but how could I have let this happen?

We called the ambulance and they took her to the local hospital. She had been denied the opportunity for our "spa day," and had she been capable of noticing, she would have been so embarrassed about how unkempt she looked as she lay on the examining table. My sister was with me along with my uncle, my brother-in-law, and my husband. We spent the next twenty-four hours in the hard chairs of the ER. Granny was still the sweetest person. Even when she was writhing in pain, she constantly apologized to the doctors and nurses for moving when they tried to start an IV, for yelling out in pain when they had to move her to another bed, or for any other simple thing she thought might have caused someone else to be inconvenienced. She had always been that way, caring and meek. She was like an innocent child, and she was physically helpless.

For years I had repeatedly shied away from opportunities to be bold in my faith, but this event changed everything. I could not stand to hear her suffer. I didn't care who was in the room or who might be offended. I knew what she needed. I knew who to call! I grabbed her hand and leaned over her. "Granny, do you want me to pray for you?" She allowed her head to plop down on her pillow as she looked up at me and said, "Yes, Jesus I believe." Really? Just like that she claimed it. Her actions weren't out of character for her, nor did they surprise me. The question was for myself. Was I even capable of calling on the Lord and ushering in His healing presence? She was such a great Christian, and while I tried to be, I failed all the time. Regardless, I knew the Word and it was life. I prayed for her, and she very calmly drifted to sleep just like a small child when she is safe in her mother's arms. I turned to take my place on the chair beside the door and noticed the nurse in the room wiping a tear from her eye as she told me how precious Granny was. The nurse had formed that opinion of my grandmother over a few hours; I had the pleasure of being with that sweet lady my whole life.

We spent hours in the hospital and the doctors confirmed Granny had a fractured pelvis. Candy and I knew what we had to do. We would take up residency in the hospital and care for her just like she had done for so many in her lifetime, and just like we had promised Papa we would always do. The first few nights were daunting and revealed a harsh truth to us girls. One night in particular, she was in and out of sleep. Part of that was due to extreme exhaustion and trauma, part was due to the medication they had squeezed into her IV. Candy and I looked at her and then at each other, both of us knowing we had a lot to discuss, but both of us were incapable of starting that very tough conversation. The hands on the clock ticked and the sound it made became the music we were forced to hear- second after second, hour after hour.

All at once, Granny opened her eyes and made conversation as if we were little girls again visiting her house. "Babies, I have more cover in the closet if y'all need it. I don't know what all is in the cabinets, but I'll fix you something to eat if you're hungry." A part of me wished I could shake myself and wake from a much needed nap, but I wasn't asleep; Candy wasn't either. We made eye contact and forced down our emotions as we simultaneously played along. "Yes, ma'am. We aren't hungry and we are comfortable. We know where the covers are if we need them." Gosh, how I wished we were at her house. How I wished I could just go to that tall linen closet in the hallway of her tiny home and grab one of the quilts she'd made with her own hands. Oh what I would give to just be able to cover up and go to sleep, to put an end to the troubling reality that stared me right between the eyes!

We knew we wouldn't leave her, but we had children, husbands, and jobs. We had to come up with a rotation to fulfill our daily responsibilities and to be with Granny around the clock. She was our responsibility too. My uncle also had a job and lived in Jacksonville, Florida, so he had to take shifts and travel back every other weekend. My mother wasn't in good health and did not make the trip at all. That is another story I will share in another chapter.

There Granny lay, the very woman who had nursed so many church members back to health. The woman who had raised her own siblings when she was twelve years old because her parents died before her thirteenth birthday. She was now the one in need of a caretaker. We spent several days watching Andy Griffith and "working puzzles" as she always called it. She seemed to gain a little strength each day. However, her childlike mentality revealed itself a bit more each evening time. Candy and I finally found some humor by seeing who could make it to the door without her opening one eye and saying, "You ain't leaving are you, baby?" She had someone with her every hour. We committed to being there, and as she realized we meant what we promised, she relaxed and focused on getting out.

The recovery was long, and I will admit, I was less than patient with the facility and staff at times. Throughout her ministry, Granny had taken me with her to visit the elderly and we had seen the way so many were mistreated and left to starve because nobody was there to help them feed themselves. That was a huge burden to Granny. She had made a point to volunteer and she fed so many people over the years. All of those moments found their way to the forefront of my mind. I refused to leave her and take any risk of something like that happening to her.

Since she was visiting our family as an out of state guest, we had to deal with insurance issues. Who would have thought an emergency situation like this one would have meant a person had to literally battle to receive care? Additionally, we had to wait on a vacancy at various places, and I had to constantly fight the monster of guilt that tried to rear his head and bring me down. Afterall, if I hadn't left her in the family room, she would be in the hospital.

Granny managed to build a little strength, and Candy and I continued to feed her as much as she would eat. She stuck with some of her favorites like toast and jelly, grits, and jello. Soon enough, she was eating tomato soup and grilled cheese sandwiches. Things were looking up, and I loved watching her gain physical strength.

One morning as we were waiting on the physical therapist and doctor to make their rounds, Granny became quite comical as she began to show me the things she could do. She said she was ready to go home and would show them she could do what they asked her to do, and she could do it at home just as easily as in that hospital. She wiggled her right foot in a small circle, and moved her legs back and forth one at a time. She asked for the walker and very carefully reached for the rubber handles. I watched her eyebrows surge upward and her lips pursed together. Her eyes focused intently on the pale yellow wall in front of her. She raised her body from the side of the bed and stood proudly behind the walker. "See, baby. I don't need to be here. I can do all this stuff from the house. Now they don't need to keep me here another day." Oh how I wanted her to come home too, so I told her I would ask. You should have seen her eyes light up! Then, the most precious prayer began to flow from her little feeble lips. I quickly grabbed my phone to video that moment- not to post to social media, but to store in the depths of my

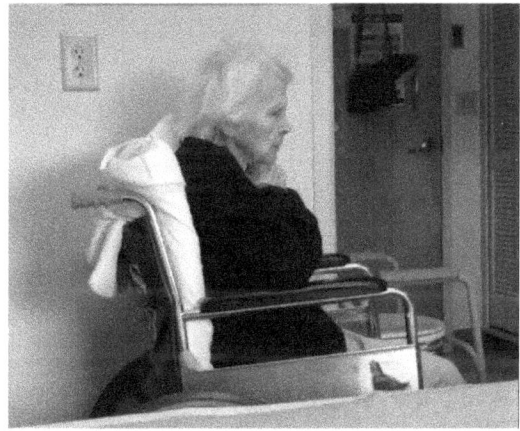

Figure 11 Granny

heart as a prime example of a Christian woman and her faith.

Around an hour later, the doctor came in and as I promised, I asked about taking Granny home. The doctor warned me there was still a lot of work to be done and respectfully, but persuasively, discussed why she should stay with twenty-four hour nurse care. I looked at her face and noticed the thin lines around her cheeks and mouth. Most of those came from a mixture of age and laughter. I replayed that sweet prayer in my mind several times. I took a deep breath and confidently asked the doctor to give me specific instructions and allow me to take her home. I couldn't deprive her of the comforts of home, even if it would be my house instead of her own. The doctor batted his eyes with a bit of a surprised reaction and agreed to help me.

Like we thought, Granny wrangled her inner strength and set out to walk without a walker and get back to her home in Florida. I admired her stubbornness and laughed at her sassy comments directed to the inanimate walker. It was nothing for her to thrust it several feet in front of her and say, "Bye walker, I won't be needing you."

Even though she was showing some physical improvements, she was also becoming more confused in the evenings. One minute she loved my dog (which she renamed Whisper) and wanted it beside her in the chair. The next minute she wasn't sure where that dog came from, but it needed to move on because she didn't like dogs on her furniture. Moments like this were humorous but also concerning. The nights were getting longer and harder for us to manage while working a full-time job and taking care of a family. We moved a twin bed in the living room for her so she could sit in the chair and watch tv or visit with family, lay in bed, see me in the kitchen, and sit by the open door on sunny days. I traded my cozy bed and the arms of my husband for the living room couch. I made the mistake of leaving her alone once, and I would not do that again.

Throughout the night she would moan and cry. I would have to figure out what she needed and wrestle with her dead weight, sleepy body to make her comfortable. Usually, that meant at least two trips to the bathroom or portable toilet. Since she only weighed about 95 pounds one would think the task would be easy. Surprisingly, I found out just how taxing such lifting and providing becomes to the caregiver. My sister, brother-in-law, and my husband also took shifts to complete our twenty-four hour care. We were all tired and ready for things to be normal again. Regardless, we all did whatever we could to make it work because she would have done the same for us.

A few weeks later, Granny was feeling better and moving around slowly, but pretty well. She was still having episodes of confusion brought on by her Dementia. However, Candy and I realized she could remember things from long ago. She could recount stories of her childhood and ours. Miraculously, she could also sing every word to hymns we sang together. I think it's worth noting two points here. First, the innocence of childhood and the emotions that accompany true love cannot be erased. Secondly, sickness is not from God. He is the healer. The mind is the devil's playground, but the spirit is God's dwelling place. Granny may not have remembered eating lunch, but she knew "Amazing Grace." How sobering to realize her worship was deeply ingrained in her spirit and no disease could take that from her. What would my spiritual archive look like if I were in her shoes? The next part of this chapter is not my favorite to write. It is very "raw" as the teenagers today would say. It is not dramatized or exaggerated. It is simply genuine.

    Granny finally got her wish and my uncle made the lonely drive to Mississippi to pick her up. She was finally going to "her home." She was thrilled and waited like a person going on a much anticipated vacation. That is all she talked about that day. She wondered how the neighbors were doing, how the weather was, and most importantly, how her yard looked. Of course she was going to miss us, but home is where she wanted to be. It was the destination for which she had longed. I, being the overly protective type, felt my heart palpitate while I caught myself clenching my jaw teeth together. Who would keep a close eye on her? Who would remind her to take her medicine and eat? I knew my uncle would be with her, but I felt like a mother needing to see to her myself. This departure was going to be very hard and I was dreading it. I wanted to be as happy as she was. I praised the Lord for her ability to overcome the obstacles she had faced, but I also worried about her. I had a connection with her that I know deep in my heart is a connection many people never experience. So there it was. The war between my faith and anxiety or fear. Yes, I know fear and anxiety are not from God, but I also know those were two very real emotions I had swelling inside me. I just didn't have a good feeling and I could not shake it no matter how hard I tried. I was like the disciples on the boat, and the storm was gaining strength.

Granny had gotten up early and we made sure she was dressed in a comfortable ash gray sweatshirt and sweatpants. She was always cold, so we layered her socks and added a Cuddl Dud shirt under the sweatshirt. I had given her a manicure and pedicure the week before, so the only thing lacking was the hairdo. Granny's hair was as soft as cotton and very, very thin. She had not allowed herself to go gray until her own children started seeing their hair turn silver. Nonetheless, she always wanted her hair styled. I kept a tiny barrel curling iron at my house for that specific purpose. As the clock ticked to late morning, my heart succumbed to a slow ache. It was time to let her go. She walked so intentionally to the truck and looked back with a huge smile on her face. We embraced again, and she said, "I don't know what I would do without my girls. I love y'all." The reality was we didn't know what we would do without her. Suddenly, all the inconsistent sleep patterns, long hours, and physical demands to care for her seemed so minuscule. As crazy as it may seem, I knew we would miss every part of that exhausting journey. There was also joy in the sweet victories we claimed, and watching her walk on her own with a smile on her face was priceless to us.

Granny was a stranger in her own house. My uncle said although she had talked incessantly about being home the entire ride back to Duval County, her confused expression overtook the fond memories and she could not remember much about the place she had called home for more than 60 years. Each day brought with it some new struggles, but again, evening proved to be worse. She had to be reminded to do the basic things- eat, take medicine, bathe. These reminders were very much contrary to the organized, stylish woman she had always been.

Not long after she was settled back in her house, I received a call I had not anticipated would come so soon. Granny was very sick again and had been taken to a hospital. I stayed in touch to offer what uplifting words I could offer. Inside, I was being torn apart. I began to feel such guilt. Why did I agree to let her go home? Then again, who was I to tell my grandmother she couldn't go to her house? Regardless, the battle in my mind intensified. I should have kept her and protected her. I know, you may be thinking what many told me repeatedly, "Even if she had been with you, the disease would have progressed." I know those words should have brought comfort, but they didn't.

A couple of weeks after she was taken to the hospital she suffered a stroke. This time, the phone conversation left me feeling like a victim of a horrible tragedy in which I had to wait for help to arrive. I was at work when I got the call. My uncle began to explain how she was not able to eat and was not really responding. He told me he would keep me informed each day. That would not be necessary. I quickly replied, "I'll see you in about eight hours. I'm on my way." I submitted my leave form and drove home. I made a call to my family to let them know what was going on, and we made our arrangements for the next few days. I gathered some random clothes and other essential items and attempted to prepare myself for another devastating reality check. The key word is attempted. I stayed in contact with my uncle throughout the day and let him know when I arrived. The facility was beautiful and serene. Granny would have loved the huge garden statue of Jesus surrounded by vines and flowering plants.

"I'm here. How do I get in?"

"Come to the side door and they will buzz you through. I have to tell you now, she is very thin and weak. It is probably going to bother you when you see her," my uncle replied. I felt my countenance drop a little as my shoulders melted downward like a candle losing its shape to the heat of the flame. Surely that was a little exaggerated; she couldn't have lost that much weight and stamina so fast.

The halls were long and uniquely shaped. Each wing of the building formed a geometrical shape. As I walked briskly, I felt my heart accelerate a few beats. My eyes began to burn, and I realized it was because I was not blinking. Instead, I had them widened as I focused on the signs adjacent to each patient's door. As I passed through the middle of one of the hallways, I noticed several of the patients sitting in their wheelchairs playing games and visiting with family. My heart twinged with the desire to share that type of moment with Granny. I took a deep breath and kept walking. Near the end of the hallway, I came to a room that had the sweetest sign outside the door. It read, "Please be mindful. Angels are ministering here." I looked on the wall above the sign and stared at the letters that formed the name- Betty L. Jones. The sign, the reverence, the patient...Granny.

My uncle met me at the door and hugged my neck. He tried to prepare me for what I was about to see. To be honest, I do not remember a word he said. I just knew the purest, most humble Christian woman was lying in a bed, and I had to get to her. I opened the door slowly and walked as if I were trying not to wake a baby. I suppose that was out of respect and habit, but Granny didn't know I was there. My eyes blurred with tears as I stepped from the end of her bed to her left side. I must have swallowed five times trying to find that inner warrior I wrote about earlier. My nose was burning from the inside down to the depths of my throat. I looked up slowly and batted my eyelashes to unlock the L'oreal dam preventing my tears from escaping freely. I used the side of my hand to dab the salty tears and took a very labored deep breath. I didn't want Granny to know I was upset. I needed to control my emotions and show strength for her.

I leaned over and softly spoke, "Hey Granny. I'm here." Her little eyes were closed and she seemed to be resting pretty comfortably. I caught myself staring at her angelic face and I managed to put on a half-smile. I had made it to her and she would know that. Like a scene from a Hallmark movie, Granny's eyelids fluttered for a second and then opened. She knew! Granny mustered up the energy to moan a little. I sat beside her and reached for her soft, thin, hands. She responded with as much of a hold as she could offer. My half smile quickly became a full-blown grin, the kind that shows expression from the lips and the eyes. I explained to Granny that we were all going to be there with her- my family and my sister's family. Granny took a breath and with the exhale her lips formed a crooked smile. The stroke had affected one side of her body. But, she knew her girls were there.

I learned a lot more about her condition that evening as I became an overprotective granddaughter once again. Not only had the stroke affected her body, it was damaged so that she could not eat without aspirating. In addition to those things, she had contracted a very deadly infection. In fact, they had not allowed anyone to visit for several days. I had already determined I would take whatever risk associated with visiting her. I would not be denied that right. In short, the odds were not in her favor at all. Her body had already begun to give in to the later stages of dementia, then the stroke, add to that the inability to eat properly, and top it with the infection. All I could do was call out to God and find peace in Him.

The medical facility was full of thoughtful, caring nurses and doctors. There was never a minute we were not checked on or given support. They made sure they brought us a cart full of fresh coffee, tea, water, and snacks every single day. Everyone learned each other's names and shifts. It was a weird experience, but it was like Granny had forced another family reunion and added more people to the group. Day after day the ladies would tell us how sweet Granny was and how she had been a blessing to them. What? So even in the midst of suffering physically, Granny had managed to enkindle the fruits of the spirit and show the love of Christ. I'm telling you, the woman was unbelievable.

Although she was frail, the minute my children made their way in the room, she pointed and smiled. Her smile was crooked. The stroke had caused paralysis in one side of her face. She didn't have to tell me that bothered her. I knew. We had shared so many conversations, prayer times, and laughs together. I felt like God was allowing me to sense things for which she could not ask. I am still astounded when I think about the examples. I noticed the way she looked at me, her eyes seemed to call me, and I made my way to her bed. As I leaned over I asked her if her mouth was bothering her. She made the slightest motion with her head and I saw her white hairs go up and down on the pillow. She was motioning Yes. I knew I had to pray for her. For one, she would have done it for me. Secondly, because I knew God would honor my request.

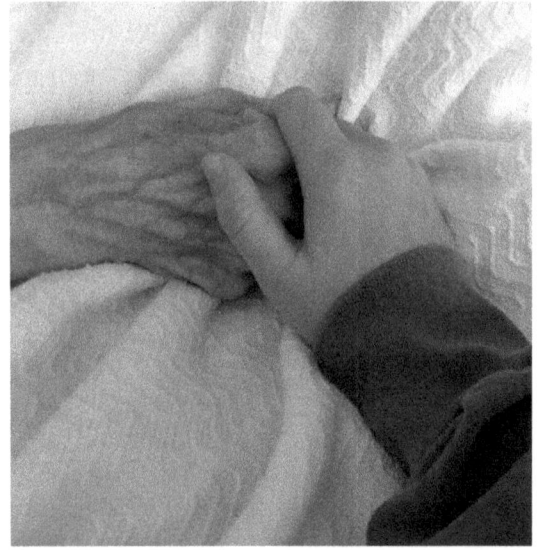

Figure 12 Granny and my hands

Minute by minute I watched her every breath rise and fall. I visited with the nurses and took on a lot of their duties because I felt like Granny deserved to be taken care of by someone who truly knew her and loved her deeply. The nurses were so kind, but kept reminding me about the dangers of coming in contact with bodily fluids, seeing stages of death that were not easily erased from one's mind, and actually watching someone die. As unexplainable as it is, I had to be there through it all. I changed her each time her body expelled toxins as it emptied itself for the last time. I watched her hands and feet take shape. I held her bony frame and tried to cough with her to help her clear her throat although I knew she was drowning in her own fluids. Each time I held her I soaked up the embrace.

Candy and I knew Granny enjoyed hearing her family sing about Jesus. She always told us to use our talent for the Lord. One afternoon as her body really began to feel the pains of death and slowly began to shut down, we leaned over her and started talking about singing some of her favorites. Without any planning whatsoever, we decided on one song.

> *"Jesus, Jesus, Jesus, there's just something about that name. Master, Savior, Jesus, like the fragrance after the rain. Jesus, Jesus, Jesus, let all heaven and earth proclaim. Kings and kingdoms will all pass away, but there's something about that name."*

The song brought her rest and brought us peace. There is no other name like the name of Jesus. The soft sounds of our voices echoed in the room and I envisioned what it would be like when she met Jesus.

Day after day I watched her sleep. At the change of each shift, the nurses discussed the various stages of death and explained what we could expect. In the most ridiculous way, I embraced every single moment I had with her. I told her what a wonderful person she was and how much I appreciated everything she had done for me. I knew hearing was the last sense to leave the body, and I wanted to make sure she heard me tell her how much I loved her and appreciated what she had been in my life.

Like clockwork, I knew when she needed her mouth swabbed, when she needed more medicine, or when she just wanted to hear us talk to her. Strangely, as I kissed her cheek, I noticed she began to smell like a baby - that baby formula lingering on the lips smell. Candy noticed the same thing. When one of the nurses came in (we had the same nurses at this point), we shared our discovery with her. She actually teared up and made a very big deal about it. She told us that most people never notice that and it takes someone who is really in sync with a loved one to notice. It wasn't a stench. It was just a light smell but it was another sign of death.

One night Candy and I were with her and the nurse had given us her stats. She was going for long periods of time without taking a breath and her pulse was nearly gone. She kept having episodes where we just knew it was over, but her body would jolt and she would take a breath. It was painful for her, and painful to watch. Her eyes would pop open, and it resembled something from a horror movie. We were very uneasy about it and everyone seemed baffled. I asked the Lord to help her and allow her body to rest. As I sat curled up in a corner, I remembered something. Granny had a pacemaker. I quickly pushed the nurse button and gave the hospice nurse the information. A team of nurses came to the room a few minutes later and explained that type of pacemaker was, for lack of better terms, kickstarting her heart every time it stopped. The solution was to place a large, round, heavy magnet over the pacemaker. With that, I made one of the hardest decisions of my life. I would place the magnet over her heart; I could not let someone else do it. There is no way to describe the emotions I dealt with, but I also felt a duty to keep her from suffering. Once the magnet was in place, the episodes ceased. Granny, however, still had faint vitals. I believe it was a divine intervention to give me confirmation that I had done what was right. She was still alive; I didn't cause her heart to stop completely.

The clock kept ticking. One of the custodians was cleaning down the hall and came to check our room. She had an angelic voice and sang hymns the entire time she was in the room. Our family talked about how beautiful that was and how comforting for patients and family members. Afterwards, our husbands told us they believed Granny was hanging on because she didn't want us to see her give in. Remember, she had always told us to stand up, be strong, and never give up. It took a lot of convincing on my husband's part, but deep down, I knew he was probably right. The guys dropped us off at the hotel and they took the night shift. It was the first time I had been away from her. Early the next morning, my phone rang. I jumped up and answered it. "She's gone baby." I looked at my children with tears in my eyes. They knew she had made it to her final destination. Granny was in Heaven with Jesus and would be waiting for us to meet her there one day.

When I arrived back at the hospital and made my way to her, I wept. I also noticed something spectacular. God says we will not have any sickness or sadness when we are with Him. God did honor my prayer request. Granny's face was no longer drawn to the side. Her mouth was normal. She was healed.

I've already mentioned how beautiful the hospital was, but I have to end this chapter with one more precious gem. The hospital honored Granny as a preacher's wife and child of God. The nurses and doctors very ceremoniously lined up and patients lined the halls. We walked behind the adorned cart carrying her body, and Granny was given a parade of sorts as she was taken out of the building. A voice so clear and angelic sang a beautiful song for the entire facility to hear. When I turned my head to follow the sound, I recognized the source. It was the custodian. She led the team and in the most reverent way escorted Granny and family outside.

Chapter Thirteen
Empty Toilet Paper Rolls

This chapter is one I have laughed about over and over again. I tried to dismiss it because it really is quite silly. However, maybe that's the point. Oftentimes we have to be jarred by the simple, silly things in life to make us see our purpose. Bear with me as I try to explain how simple, ugly, bare toilet paper rolls spoke volumes to me.

For at least four years (seriously, four years) I noticed every time I went to a restroom, the brown, cardboard toilet paper roll was peeping through the last soft square of tissue. The first time it happened, I did what I do at home. I grabbed another roll of toilet paper and replaced the empty roll with a fresh roll of soft paper. This same order of events went on and on for a while until I walked in a restroom at work one day only to find the bare, brown roll. I mumbled to myself, "How hard is it to put a new roll on?" Again, I put the fresh roll of tissue on the contraption and carried on about my day. No joke, I continued to experience this same thing over and over and over. Some days I replaced the tissue without even thinking. Some days I debated doing it because I thought, "I am not their mother! How lazy can people be?" Some days I wondered how long their own homes go with a roll of toilet paper resting atop the toilet paper holder because nobody wanted to complete the simple, necessary task. After a few months of this crazy episode, I began to notice it was happening no matter where I went. I thought if I moved around from stall to stall or place to place, surely somebody else was helping replace toilet paper on the holders. How wrong was I! I kid you not, for at least four years I have been stopped in my tracks with this ridiculous household chore. Sam's, work, the mall, the movie theater, my house- if I went, the "chore" awaited me. I finally began laughing about it and even said to myself quite often, "Of course there isn't any left, Sandy is here to change it."

January 6, 2019, I went to my church to enjoy the first Sunday service of the new year. During our meet and greet I made my way to the ladies' room. You guessed it! I reached out to empty the last bit of the toilet paper off the roll and kind of chuckled to myself. As I looked at the roll with small fragments of tattered paper still somewhat adhered to the cardboard, I stood there staring as the lesson I had missed all this time became profoundly clear to me. "What are you doing to prepare the way for others? What are the essentials people need but you are griping about? Are you happy to help give others something they need? " Whoa! So for at least four long years the Lord kept putting me in a situation to change a stupid toilet paper roll, and I had managed to ignore it, change it out of habit- with no thought at all, complain about it, judge others because of it, and laugh at myself for being the "all-time toilet paper changer of the world." Not once had I ever seen it as a necessary task to prepare the place for someone else, to provide a simple something for others. I pondered on that lesson all afternoon.

The metaphor kept getting richer and richer. I realized how

insignificant my mundane task had been. Yes, I get it. It's just a toilet paper roll. But, do we really get it? Are we happy to plant seeds for the growth of others? Are we eager to do a small task even though it will not be recognized publicly? Are we even concerned about the well-being of those coming up behind us? Would we rather complain and find fault in what others don't do or don't know when we could have laid the foundation for them? My goodness, what a revelation for me! I have children of my own and two granddaughters. I have a huge responsibility to make sure I leave things for them to build upon. Our communities and churches are filled with people in need. Some people have bigger needs than others, but everyone has essential needs. Man, how quickly the Lord put me in check. Not one person is without a need for basic things. God provides for us, yet we must be willing to take on our role as leaders, mentors, and spiritual "housekeepers."

That lesson comes to mind frequently. I have been guilty of being too busy or thinking it is not my job to replenish toilet paper in every restroom I enter. Chuckle with me on that comment, but also let it sink in. It is my job. It is our job to do everything as though doing it unto Christ. Little things lead to bigger things. "If you are faithful with the little things, He will make you ruler of more" (Matthew 25:23).

Not everyone has to write a book, get on a big stage, pastor a church, serve at a summer camp, or witness in a foreign country; however, everyone is required to share his or her testimony. We are His hands and feet, so our testimony- even if it is to just one person-is life and hope. "We overcome by the word of our testimony" (Revelation 12:11). When we share our testimony, we share hope, love, and we help others overcome. Let my humorous recap of replenishing toilet paper offer you confirmation that our Lord will speak to us in whatever way He can to get our attention. Let the story also serve as a reminder that your testimony could very well be the bridge to help someone else. If you are that person, I pray you will pass along your testimony too. Take care of the little tasks and be mindful of the foundation you are building for others.

Chapter Fourteen
Satan Loves A Slough

According to the Oxford Dictionary, a slough is "a swamp; a situation characterized by lack of progress." Ironically, the word slough can also be pronounced differently and refers to shedding of skin like a snake (Dictionary.com). It's only fitting to discuss the swamp and lack of progress along with the shedding of skin as I continue my metaphor and recount some of the difficult times in my life.

One of the things I have to work on is my stubborn nature. At times, that trait has given me the grit I needed to make it through tough circumstances without giving up. Other times, that trait has compounded my struggle and intensified the pain. Regardless of what adventure life takes me on, I try to keep moving forward without allowing myself to become still, like a stagnant slough. I haven't always managed that very well.

As loving as I have described my grandparents, I must also be honest about how the enemy attacked my family. My grandparents served others relentlessly. As I have mentioned before, they were beautiful examples of Christlike love and faith. My mother grew up singing and playing the piano. My uncle grew up singing and playing any instrument he picked up. Both my mom and my uncle had God-given musical talents. Mom and Papa recorded an album and traveled with many gospel quartets. After my dad passed away, my mom continued to help with the music ministry. Like most women who lose a husband, emotionally, she had good days and bad days. She found herself in a spiral of heartache and at times, she questioned why things happened the way they did. She knew she should not question.

Like the majority of us, she knew, and had been reminded by others, she was human and should not question God. I've thought about that numerous times myself. I've been guilty of questioning God too, even if I did not say it aloud. If we are being perfectly honest, God already knows what we are thinking, feeling, harboring, and letting go. God is certainly the omnipotent one. He is all-knowing and has everything in my life under control; however, as a human- a sinner fallen from grace, I have learned in those moments, God understands my pain and my human frailty. He does not give me the greenlight to constantly question Him; to question is the opposite of trusting Him. However, I have a different opinion from many when it comes to questioning death, abuse, etc. I believe God allows us to work through those painful moments via questioning and searching for answers. It is only when we allow our raw emotions, no matter how ugly they are, to surface, that we also open ourselves to the ability to feel the love and peace of our God. We are so desperate to know an answer until we usually listen, feel, and ponder the revelation He gives. On the contrary, we must be careful as we know the devil is always lurking and waiting to attack us in those vulnerable moments. It is truly a time to be "in tune" with and rely on God completely.

Mom knew in her heart she could live a godly life and see my dad again one day, but the devil also knew her pain. When we question we allow ourselves to become raw, open flesh. At that point, the enemy takes aim and begins to work on our minds, our bodies, and our spirits. My mom remarried more than once. Each time she married I watched her battle emotionally. She was searching for that companionship, the love my dad gave her. True, God was willing to be those things for her, but mom could not find the strength within herself to fully fight off the enemy. One marriage lasted twelve years before her husband moved us to a completely different state only to begin drinking again. As the alcoholic strongholds imprisoned him, he found comfort in the arms of another woman. My mom was devastated. She had given up everything she owned, her entire life roots to move to Mississippi with this man. I watched my mom cry for days at a time. I heard my mom call out to God. I also heard her sneer angry words as she slowly folded to the destructive grip of depression. My beautiful mother stopped seeing herself as talented, attractive, and important. She hurt so deeply. I was sixteen, and I could not really understand her pain. She learned to hide it well as she pushed me harder to plan for my future. When I was seventeen, I graduated high school. I had been able to double up on my required subjects and skip the eleventh grade. I did not like Mississippi at all, so I wanted out of high school as fast as I could get out. Mom was proud of me, but mom was not herself.

Soon after my graduation, I began working and going to

college. Mom decided to move back to Jacksonville. I toyed with the idea of leaving, but coursework would not transfer easily, and I knew I could not make it work. I stayed. I was seventeen years old working two jobs and going to college. Most children look for freedom and can hardly wait to be on their own. My freedom did not feel very free. Deep down I carried a burden for my mom. In the deepest part of my heart I felt like I had been abandoned. I understood her need to get back to Granny and Papa; I understood her need to go home. Unfortunately, I yearned for home too, but I knew I could not go. I continued to focus on my education and balance the two jobs as best I could. Eventually, I was able to get a job at Walmart so I could keep an ok income with one place of employment. An ok income meant I still had an extremely tight budget, but I had more employee benefits. I was still eating more ramen noodles than I care to remember, and I was still considering a can of cold vegetables a delicacy. Nonetheless, I never went hungry. I earned every penny I spent, and I learned to appreciate some of the smaller "luxuries" in life like free walks in a park, crafting with things found in nature, family time, and good health.

Navigating through those years alone was not easy, but it forced me to become strong and independent. My mom's health declined and she never really regained her purpose. She lost the sense of belonging and allowed herself to live in the trap devised by evil. She was worth more than she believed. She gave in to living a very stressful life and felt like that's just what she was supposed to have. She knew better! That's the part that still bothers me. It saddens me to admit it, but it also reminds me of how quickly Satan will attach himself to the minds of God's children. He loves a slough, and he will do his very best to keep us in the muck as long as possible. Mom still believed in God, but like many others, she had been deceived and settled for a life when she could have had so much more.

Sandy Reid

Chapter Fifteen
Taproots of Faith

I was young when I married the love of my life, and we started a family right away. We were both excited to become parents even though we had no idea what all that might entail. I had always loved kids, so I wanted at least four children. I never imagined carrying my first child would be so difficult. I had been a very active person, and I assumed I would be able to carry and birth children without any major issues. I was wrong. It only took a few weeks for me to become extremely sick. Almost immediately after my eyes opened in the mornings, I began the horrendous cycle of being hungry, eating, and vomiting up anything I tried to hold down. I had absolutely no energy. Morning sickness was not a morning thing for me. I was sick morning, noon, and night. It was absolutely exhausting and brought with it zero joy. I was put on bedrest the last few weeks of pregnancy, and I had gained over 70 pounds. Like most women during their last trimester, my emotions were far and wide, and so was my nose! My sweet husband would tell me how beautiful he thought I was, and all I could do was wail and say, "You are just saying that. My nose is huge."

Women do have to go through a lot during pregnancy, but let me just take a moment to acknowledge the poor husbands who have to endure the rollercoaster ride of emotions. They do not have a chance. The beast we become is unlike anything they have ever encountered. Now, the humorous part of these truths is that some women and men put themselves through all of this more than once! Do not get me wrong, children are a blessing, and we put ourselves through all of that because they are worth it. But, we have to admit, it's the perfect example of antithesis. Thankfully, I managed to carry our baby full term. In fact, I carried her longer than I should have. I began experiencing labor and with a mixture of nerves and excitement, my husband and I went to the hospital. We made that trip more than once. I was given medication to stop contractions and sent home. We walked and walked and walked. We were young and naive so we followed the directions of the medical team. Lesson learned: always ask questions and listen to your body. I agonized in full labor for days. Eventually, things were not good at all and we found ourselves admitted, monitored, and quickly taken back to have an emergency C-section.

Our sweet baby girl's heartbeat was stopping and I was very sick. My temperature was rising, my husband was panicking, and my heart was pounding. I will never forget the look on the doctor's face when he asked me my due date. To say he was angry about me being sent home time and time again would be an understatement. I could tell we were in a serious situation. "We are about to have a baby," he said. No longer did he finish those words when a team of people filled the room. They were strapping things on me, pushing tubes in me, and rolling me to the coldest, most sterile place I have ever been. I remember scanning the room and seeing steel everywhere. Then, I remember seeing the bright sun-like light as the doctor positioned it over my belly. "Can you feel this, Mrs. Reid?" One nurse asked me as she placed a cold instrument on my leg. No, I could not feel it. I couldn't feel anything. I stared into the light trying to catch a glimpse of what was going on. Sick, I know, but for whatever reason I always try to see what someone is doing to me, especially if it involves blood or surgical equipment. I remember looking at my husband and asking if he was ok. He was so strong, but I know he was so afraid. My body began to move the table, and he still recalls how terrible it was to try to talk to me while he saw the doctor's muscles flexed as he pulled back layers of my stomach and called for various surgical tools. The team moved in like an army of ants overtaking an unattended meal. Within minutes, they were moving about so quickly I had no idea what was going on. I listened intently. Silence. All I could hear was the swishing sound of the sterile, disposable surgical team coats and lots of numbers being called out.

I tried to focus again and listen. Silence. At that moment, a nurse came by me with our baby girl and did a small dip down move. "See her mama, here she is." I saw her sweet little face and noticed the distinct wrinkle across the top of her nose. I never heard her cry. She wasn't moving at all. Lights out! That is all I remember.

Meanwhile, my poor husband had been told to go out and let the family know the baby had been born. He was a brand new dad, and the family was eagerly awaiting the arrival of our princess. My brother-in-law stood with the video camera ready to capture the moment when daddy and little girl came through the oversized hospital doors. They waited. Finally, Chris came through the door. He wasn't holding a newborn baby wrapped in a swaddle. He was alone and shared the news that our baby was born, but was quickly taken to NICU.

As if the day had not been devastating enough for a young, new dad, when Chris came back to see me, his heart dropped. I was lying there perfectly still in the large, cold room. He came up to me and I didn't open my eyes. He tried to talk to me, but he only heard the shuffling of feet outside the area. Tears began to fall, and in that moment he thought he had also lost his wife. The urgent tasks that monopolized the focus of the team of nurses forbade them the opportunity to explain to Chris that they had put me to sleep. Isn't it amazing that even the medical professionals know how powerful the connection is between a mother and her child? To know it is better to give a mother some medication to keep her from realizing what is happening with her newborn serves as proof that God created women to nurture and protect their own-even if it puts their own life at risk.

Fortunately, someone noticed Chris was upset and quickly consoled him with the facts of what had occurred. He was able to exhale a bit of relief and girded himself for the report from the NICU doctors.

When I finally licked my dry lips and attempted to open my eyes, I felt a deep, sharp pain in my belly. The agony was so great I gasped for air and widened my eyes. I was forced to remember where I was, no doubt. The nurse explained to me she had to "massage" my uterus to make sure I didn't hemorrhage. I still argue that it was anything but a massage. That torture continued until I finally reached up and firmly grabbed the wrist of the nurse and in my medicated stupor growled, "Do not touch me again. Show me how and I will do it myself." I am always a good patient, but I had been in labor for two weeks, had an emergency C-section, had only laid eyes on my baby for a millisecond, had been medicated to a drunken state, so the uterus massage was the last straw. For the record, I did apologize to the nurse when I saw her a day later.

Around 1:00 in the morning, the neonatologist came in to give us an update on our little one. I suppose they knew my meds were wearing off and Chris and I were going to have a lot of questions. The first bit of news was to explain everything that happened. Next, he told us she was on oxygen but would slowly come off that as they monitored her. She was being given lots of things intravenously, as was I. He stressed the importance of breast milk and wasn't sure if or how we would make that work. Say no more! I was ready to see my girl. I would have plenty of time to practice since she would be in NICU for at least 14 days…or so they said.

Chris and I felt like we had been in a whirlwind, but the strength we provided each other was something I will always cherish. The first time we were able to visit her was one of the most precious moments of my life. She was a tiny little bundle with dark hair and I recognized that little wrinkle on her nose. Her diaper seemed humongous. She had tubes and monitors all over the place. But, she was alive. She was mine. I still remember the first time she wrapped her finger around mine. Honestly, I had so much fluid buildup, my finger looked like a balloon. Her teeny fingers lay softly on my skin. At last, we were connected again.

There was no doubt she had her daddy wrapped! He could not keep his eyes off of her, and she recognized his voice every time he spoke to her. Like many men have to do, Chris slept on the infamous chair bed. We were young, not poor- but not much past that- and he had to work. He was so exhausted, but each day he napped on and off before heading out to work the night shift . The nurses told me they would just give Kirsten a bottle since I had a lot of things going on healthwise. They didn't like the idea of me walking back and forth to the NICU. I did appreciate the thoughtfulness, but I was determined to see and touch my baby. I would feed her and pray over her, regardless of the amount of time or pain it took me to get to her. The struggle was real! I held my breath as I squirmed around enough to grab the bedrail and pull up. Once I figured out how to wrap all of my IV tubes around and stabilize myself, I inched my way down the long, glossy hallway. I kept one hand on the wall to give myself direction and compensate for the lightheaded feeling. Slowly but surely I made my way past the first turn into the straight yellow hallway that led me to my girl. Day after day, every two hours, I would make that walk to nurse her. She couldn't latch, so I would have to pump and use a tiny bottle to feed her. The process was a bit unnerving because I felt like maybe I was doing something wrong, but I kept doing it anyway. By the time I cuddled her and made it back to my room, it seemed it was time to go back to the

NICU. It did not strike me as a burden; it was part of my purpose. After a few days, the nurses moved me to a different room; I guess it was my hospital hotel. I was not leaving until I could bring my baby with me. Surprisingly, they accommodated the request.

On the tenth day of our stay, Chris had gone to work and I was getting ready to visit Kirsten. I remember this day so vividly. As I stood in the bathroom I looked in the mirror and said these words aloud, "Jesus, I thank you for my baby. She is not mine Lord; she is yours." I promise you within two minutes of my profession, I heard a knock at the door. "Mama, we have a delivery for you. Your baby is doing so well we are going to let her stay in the room with you." Have I told you how awesome God is? I was elated! I snuggled with her all afternoon and cried as I watched her latch for the first time.

We were discharged a few days later, and finally brought our girl home. She was so special to us and we knew she was a gift from God. Remember, I wanted at least four children; I have two. Shortly after having Kirsten, I began to experience more health issues. I was diagnosed with endometriosis and adenomyosis. By the time I was twenty three years old, the doctors were discussing my options with me. None of those options were promising. I had a few minor surgical procedures, but to no avail. I was heartbroken. My OBGYN discussed the final procedure- a hysterectomy. No. more. babies. I cried and prayed and cried some more. I kept hearing the words my doctor used to console me, "At least you have one child. Some people can't have one." He was right, but it didn't stop my mama heart from hurting. I focused on my little one and poured as much positive energy and Christian values in her as I could. We already knew she was special, but to hear her talk to God was so special. Her prayers were intense and she always lifted her head and looked up, eyes opened as she spoke to God.

One day she and I were playing and she asked me how people get brothers and sisters. I think I held my breath for a brief moment and thought, "Oh no! It's the question." I wasn't ready to explain that or deal with the fact she wouldn't be having any siblings. I replied the best way I knew how at that time. "God gives children to mamas and daddies." She smiled and seemed to be perfectly content. Whew! That wasn't so bad. All of the sudden, she began walking to her room. I asked her where she was going to which she quickly replied, "To ask God for a baby brother." What had I done? Oh no! I felt a twinge of fear and sadness prick my heart. I was reminded of childlike faith and how I had experienced such. Within a few minutes, she came back to the living room. The news she delivered was prophetic even though I didn't claim it at the time. "Mom, I am going to have a baby brother and his name is going to be Elijah." That was so precious, but totally out of nowhere!

Several months later, it was time to take care of my labs for surgery. My doctor wanted the routine bloodwork done the day before. He planned to go over everything with me one last time before the day of the procedure. Needles have never bothered me, so the lab procedure was uneventful. Next, I waited with papers in hand. Soon my name would be called and the process of dismantling my womb would be underway.

When the doctor came in he brought a couple of nurses with him. He was looking at the chart, and I noticed his eyebrows were scrunched up. "Good afternoon, Mrs. Reid. We have you scheduled for surgery tomorrow. I see we have your labs here, but we aren't going to be able to complete the surgery." I thought to myself, "What? Ok, I had prepared myself for this. I had completed the labs, and now I have to put this off?" "Mrs. Reid, we can't complete the surgery because the labs show you are pregnant." The nurses and doctor smiled simultaneously, and all I could do was breathe quickly and feel the warm tears drip from my eyes. "Oh my God! I can't believe this. Thank you!"

Immediately, I knew. The words Kirsten spoke were prophetic. Her childlike faith had moved God. She really was going to have a sibling! I couldn't wait to tell her. But…she also said a brother and she had named him. Was all of that prophetic? Nonetheless, I was thrilled to share the good news.

The entire pregnancy was healthy and different from the first. I thanked God daily for our baby and laughed here and there as I thanked him for allowing me to have a "normal" pregnancy and even miss out on morning sickness. I was able to work every day and Kirsten loved talking to my tummy. Finally the day came to have an ultrasound. Kirsten wanted to be there and reminded us, "I want to go so I can see my baby brother." I know I should have had unwavering faith, but I can't take credit for that. I did not. Doubt began to creep in my thoughts. "What if you take her and it's a girl?

How will you explain this to a four year old? Are you really going to believe she knows it's a boy?" I recognized that doubt. I knew it was not from God. If God had done all the things I've written about thus far, He would do this too. Kirsten sat on her daddy's lap facing the screen. I prepared my bare belly for the gooey gel the nurse would squirt on top. The nurse moved the instrument around a few times, and found baby Reid. As we listened to the heartbeat, the nurse said, "Are you ready to see if you are having a brother or sister?" Without hesitation, Kirsten replied, "I already know I'm having a brother. His name is Elijah." Chris and I locked eyes. We both knew we had to trust God in the process- whatever this process was. The nurse clicked various buttons and explained the heart rate, skeletal system, and some other things. As only God's humor can do, the baby was lying with both hands behind his head and with his legs opened wide. "Well, there is no doubt you are having a little brother." The nurse could not control her laughter as used high-tech equipment to type BOY above the manhood. "I told you." Kirsten said with a huge smile. Again, I felt the warmth of my tears as they slid down the sides of my face and into my hair. How and why did I ever allow one moment of doubt? Once again, God had shown Himself faithful and true. The miracle we were experiencing was life changing for us and extremely beneficial for Elijah's big sister.

    Elijah Reid was born on March 4th. He was a healthy baby boy. Everything about the delivery was textbook, and the nurses made sure mom and dad experienced a normal childbirth. Both of my children (everyone's children) are a gift from God, and I am so grateful He used my babies to teach me more about His love and faithfulness.

I now know the significance and strength of these growing pains would be needed over two decades later.

Sandy Reid

Chapter Seventeen
He is Faithful

It is true what they say about grandchildren; they are grand! I have two beautiful granddaughters and both are miracles in their own way. I'll give a quick synopsis of both. I was traveling for work, and as usual, I had my music playing loudly. I listened to a few sermons and then began to worship as I drove. I love to worship while I drive. While I was away, I visited the local mall; it was close enough to Christmas, and I also love to shop. I started feeling moved to look for certain items. Everything I was drawn to was about God's faithfulness. I had no idea why, but I followed His lead. I purchased several items over the course of a few days.

One item was a small painting of an old church with the lyrics, "Great is thy faithfulness" brushed across the canvas. I visited a bookstore, of course, and found a book and a frame that had the word Believe on it. It had a small clip to which you could attach a picture and change it out from year to year. When I purchased the frame I started to get a strange feeling that my daughter was expecting. I didn't let the thought linger, but I also couldn't keep it from returning. I would be thrilled, but I wasn't going to ask her about it. She and her husband wanted a child, but her body had not been cooperating and she was troubled. I made my purchases and took them home.

A few days later, I made some last minute additions to my

Christmas decorations and started preparing for my favorite time of year. I smiled as I placed my new frame on the mantle. At the time I thought it was the whole "believe in Christmas" theme I had going on as it looked so adorable with my snowy decor. The tin letters really looked nice with the warm white lights. Kirsten called and said she and her husband were coming over and they had a Christmas gift they needed to give us. I thought nothing of it since my daughter has never been good at making someone wait for a gift.

When they arrived, she handed us a small box and told us to go ahead and open the gift. We made a joke about her inability to keep a secret and pulled back the tab on the box. Inside we found a pacifier and handwritten note letting us know we may need the paci at our house when our grandbaby visited with us. Chris and I were absolutely thrilled! We were going to be grandparents and God had given them the desire of their heart.

Eager to have her first official visit, Kirsten made an appointment with her OBGYN. She was so excited to be a mother. I put in a full work day and received a call on my way home. At the other end of the line I could hear the crack in Kirsten's voice. She pushed through the crying to tell me the doctor sent her home and told her to prepare for a miscarriage. My warrior spirit took over. Oh no, not on my watch! I promptly told her we were not going to receive or accept that report. I continued to offer encouragement even though I knew it was probably hard for her to absorb. From that moment on, I began claiming life. I spoke to her womb and called her body to line up with the word. I claimed scripture every day. God cannot lie and I reminded Him daily. Other people did not offer the same support. They told her they were sorry and how to handle the experience because they had dealt with miscarriage. One person even bought a "gift" ornament to memorialize the baby. As soon as Kirsten told me, I advised her to get rid of that item and to not accept any calls or words from anyone negative. We didn't have time to play; we were in a spiritual battle. It is vital to surround yourself with likeminded people, especially when you need to be encouraged.

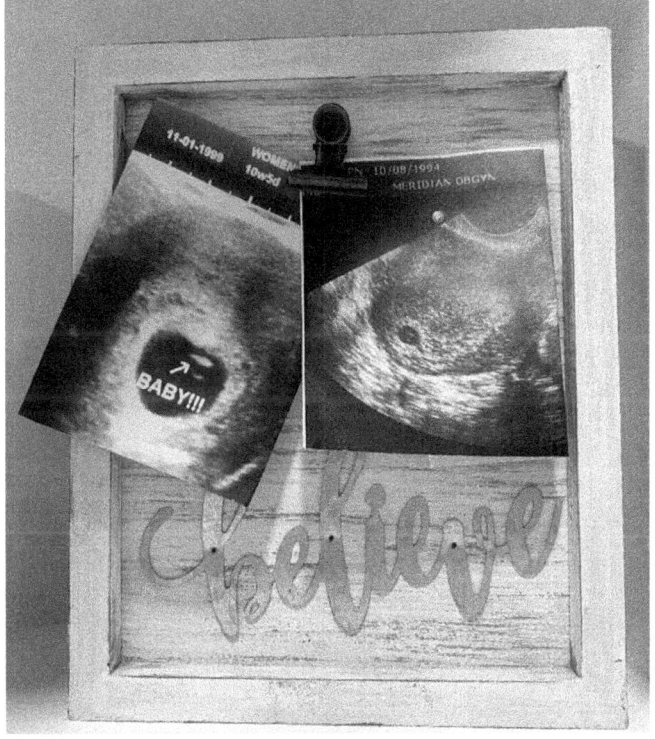

Figure 13 Ultrasound

When she brought the ultrasound picture to show me, I made a copy and knew exactly where it belonged. I trimmed the edges and carefully placed the black and white photo that detailed our little rice-shaped baby in the newly purchased "Believe" frame. This frame was a constant reminder to stand firm in faith and believe God would see us through. Days turned into weeks, and weeks turned into months. Our sweet miracle was no longer the size of a grain of rice, and Kirsten didn't miscarry. My first granddaughter was a healthy baby growing quickly in her mama's womb. When September came, we welcomed our little gift from God. I am so thankful for a God that answers prayers and gives us little ones to love. He trusts us to raise them to bring glory to Him.

Several years later, my son and daughter-in-law announced they were expecting a baby. I would do a poor job of expounding to you the surge of joy that announcement brought with it, so I won't even try. Having one granddaughter was absolutely wonderful. I couldn't imagine what having two grandchildren would be like.

Baby and mama were growing and changing as expected. We hosted a baby reveal and found ourselves extremely surprised when pink confetti filled the air. Life as a Honey (my grandparent name) was getting sweeter by the minute! We planned a family trip to the beach and started capturing photographs of Kelsey's baby bump. I, of course, went into full-blown shopping mode. I didn't need much of a reason to shop, but a new granddaughter definitely gave me a green light.

Five months in, Kelsey started experiencing sickness and complications. She had dealt with female issues for a long time, so the pain she was experiencing didn't give her any reason to believe she was in labor. One summer night, Elijah left for work and Kelsey tried to rest. She found herself struggling to hold down food or drink. Then she realized the pain was not going away; in fact, it was increasing in duration. Following those things there was a new development- blood, lots of blood. She contacted Elijah and he made it to her as quickly as he could. Kirsten met them at the hospital and called us to let us know what was going on.

Once we arrived, we learned Kelsey was already 6cm dilated. She was in labor, and the doctors and nurses were trying to stop the process. She was not far enough along to give birth to a healthy baby. If we heard that once, we heard it a hundred times. Kelsey was such a trooper. She embraced "mama bear" mode and did whatever it took to try to keep the baby from coming too soon. Medications to stop labor, to prevent dehydration, and to calm both mama and baby were quickly attached to the IV pole and pumped in Kelsey's veins. We rallied the troops and people from everywhere began to pray. We needed a miracle.

The hospital room became home for a few days. As a precaution, the doctors ordered specific medication to help the baby's lungs and brain develop faster. They turned Kelsey's bed so her head was facing downward, which would help alleviate any pressure on the uterus. She was absolutely miserable, stuck staring at the ceiling for three long days, but she was a fighter. At one point, I leaned over to check on her and noticed her eyes were so swollen she could barely see. As I retreated to my chair, I quietly called out to God. It was so hard to see her so miserable. My mama heart didn't like watching her suffer.

Every time I opened my phone or read my bible, a new scripture was there to confirm God was with us. I held on to each one. Kirsten took on the role of making sure everyone had clean clothes and food to eat. As she was leaving one night, she saw the most beautiful rainbow located directly over the hospital room. She claimed that as her sign God had everything under control. She shared the picture with us, and we all agreed the rainbow was a symbol for us. I appreciate doctors and nurses and have great respect for them; however, I do believe God transcends all. The next few paragraphs are a mere snapshot of the actual moments, but I am sure I will write more about this event in the future.

The baby was not obeying the rules; she was coming regardless of what the doctors tried to do. Kelsey was 23 weeks pregnant. The neonatologist came in to discuss the situation. What we heard infuriated me as a mom and even more so as a believer.

"Some things are better than death."

"Y'all are young enough to have more children."

"Even if you have her she will be like a blob of jello; she won't have skin, and she will die shortly after you give birth."

"We don't deal with babies less than 26 weeks old and that's pushing it at 26." And last, but not least, the doctors had the audacity to ask a first time mom and dad, "Do you want us to do everything we can to save her if she's alive when you deliver?"

What was I hearing? Are you kidding me? I am a realist. I am fine with telling someone the odds are stacked against them, but to hear a medical professional say such horrible things and act as if we were a waste of time was totally unacceptable. Basically, they were appalled when Kelsey told them, "Yes."

The contractions came faster and harder. A nurse came in and prepped the room for delivery. Other nurses put on their gowns and gloves and joined, some secretly complimented Kelsey for wanting to keep her baby. The head nurse walked up to Kelsey's bedside and started moving things around to get her in position. My son stood aside fighting back tears, but losing the battle. My mind flashed back to Chris on the day he thought he lost his wife and child. I refused to allow such hurt and disappointment! I walked up to Kelsey to reassure her, and I heard the nurse say, "Well, just know we've done all we can do and at this point there's nothing else we can do. I'm sorry, but sometimes this just happens." I know she wasn't the devil, but at that moment, I knew those words were not from God! Our baby was not dead, and the monitor was still showing a heartbeat! I looked Kelsey in the eyes and said in a loud, confident voice, "We know different. We do not believe a word she said."

Chris and I had to leave the room, but I knew the kids were not alone- our prayer warriors were praying, and I knew God was in that room. I put my air pods in and played "The Blessing" on repeat. The words of that song are straight from God's word and they are so powerful. I began to walk up and down that hall calling forth scripture and praying in my heavenly language. People tried to talk to me and stop me in the hallway, but I kept going. I was locked in and at war. I could feel the presence of God, and I refused to believe the report the doctors gave.

Within minutes, the hospital room door opened and the neonatologist and his team came running down the hall pushing an incubator. I looked as they came toward me, and I saw a tiny leg in the air. Then, I saw the leg kick and the itty bitty arms wiggle. Praise God! I wasn't looking at a blob of jello; I was looking at a baby! I saw fully formed limbs AND pink skin. I could have run through the entire hospital! It didn't matter to me that she still had a long road ahead. I knew in my heart the Lord had just performed a miracle and there was no way he would leave us now. Nobody could or can tell me my God isn't real!

Our baby was flown by jet to the University of Birmingham NICU where she received the best possible care. Kelsey moved to Birmingham to be with her baby every day. Elijah drove down every weekend and worked during the week. Their young lives had been uprooted and changed forever. Their faith had increased tremendously, and our prayer warriors continued to lift them up. God had already used this baby to move in the lives of so many people and He continues to reveal Himself through her. There were good days and bad days, but we knew who was in control.

They spent almost half a year in Birmingham. As God would have it, we were able to bring our baby home just in time for Christmas. Miracle Maddie Lee has given us such joy and has been a great reminder that our God still performs miracles. I realize not everyone has a story like this. I personally know some who have lost babies and have been given horrible news. My heart empathizes with those families. I do not understand or know why those things happen, but I do know God is faithful regardless. If you have a story of hope, I pray you find the courage to share it with others. If you are hurting because of a loss, I pray God will wrap you in His arms and help you heal as only He can. If you are struggling with guilt, remember guilt is not from God. No matter how many weeks or months you carried your baby, God chose you to carry that child. You are special and so are the children he gives us. Continue to seek God and be honest with Him about your feelings (he knows anyway). The Bible says He is the great comforter. I challenge you to accept that and allow Him to heal your brokenness and use it for His glory.

Sandy Reid

Chapter Eighteen
Which Lion Do You Follow?

Right in the midst of the celebration of our precious miracle granddaughter turning one, Hell unleashed its demons on my family again. I immediately realized it was an attack because anytime we give God praise and tell the good news, Satan has to try to stop it. Yet, the Lord has equipped us with the very armor we need for any battle we encounter. He has promised to be with us and fight the battles for us IF we allow Him. As my daughter received papers giving her a court date and indicating a custody battle, a quickening happened on the inside of me. If you have ever been privy to the paternal intuition and or spiritual quickening, you understand the stirring about which I am writing. If you have not experienced either of these, I will try to describe it the best way I can. The feeling is truly from the inside out. It is like an excitement mixed with a warning or sense of urgency. The warrior spirit I described in the earlier chapters of this text, began to rise up. Almost instantly, the scripture in 1 Peter came to mind.

"The devil is like a roaring lion, seeking whom he may devour." The Lord began to press upon me the words like and may. So when we see that scripture, we should see the devil is like a roaring lion. He is a counterfeit to the true Lion of the tribe of Judah. According to National Geographic, the lion's prey is generally faster than he is, but he stalks his prey before attacking. Satan stalks us. He waits for a vulnerable moment. He sneaks around and hears when we speak negatively or verbalize weakness. We must be watchful and on guard! "The devil is like a roaring lion seeking whom he may devour. He comes to kill, steal, and destroy." If he can isolate you, he can work on you. He will keep you suppressed and insecure so he can beat you down. BUT God has defeated the enemy and has called you according to His purpose!

Secondly, we see the word may. Satan cannot devour us unless we open the door or give permission. We use that word when we ask permission. May I help you? May I give you this? See, we are asking for permission. If the person says no, we do not or should not proceed.

The word tells us to, "Resist the Devil and he will flee" (James 4:7). It does not tell us to give him permission to destroy us as individuals or as a family- no matter how loud he roars! As I am typing this chapter, I do so in faith that God has gone before us and has already taken out the enemy. I refuse to allow my daughter to go through hell and lose. I refuse to see depression creep in and weigh her down. I have prayed for her before she was born and throughout her life. She is victorious because I do NOT give permission to the lying lion. From the very beginning in the book of Genesis, the word declares, "What the devil meant for evil, God is turning to good." I am claiming this word today!

A lion's roar can be heard from at least five miles away. Think about that. If the lion has to stalk us before he preys, he can't roar as it would ruin his method of attack. Consequently, the roar is one of the awesome wonders about the animal. Guess who can roar? Satan is defenseless when the Lion of the Tribe of Judah roars! We are in that pride! According to the Smithsonian Magazine, if one feels hunted or stalked by a lion, the best actions of defense are to raise one's arms about his/her head, waving them and shouting to the top of his/her lungs. Have you ever thought about what our true praise and worship does? It unleashes our protector!

2 Chronicles 20:22 reads, "And when they began to sing and praise, the Lord set an ambush against the men of Ammon, Moab, and Mount Seir, who had come against Judah, so that they were routed." What happens when we praise? "The Lord inhabits the praises of His people" (Psalm 22:3). So if we are praising and truly worshiping, our father- the REAL lion- is with us. His roar can be heard from miles away because he isn't stalking; he's protecting and claiming what is His! Is praising an easy task when life has kicked us in the teeth? No, but is any battle ever deemed a battle if there isn't a struggle to lead to a victor?

Our praise is a weapon against the enemy. If he can stifle our praise, he can isolate us, weaken us, and prey on us. If we remember to praise and keep the word flowing from our hearts and mouths, we are promised our God is with us. Yes, it is tough sometimes. Yes, there are days you wonder if you can make it or even lift your head. Depression, isolation, suicidal thoughts, are all from the enemy to try to captivate our minds and weaken us so we feel unworthy of speaking the holy name of Jesus. Don't forget, Jesus took on all the weights and sins of the world so His children- you and I - can live freely. You MUST lift praise. Speak the name of Jesus. Resist the enemy. Say it until you believe it…even if the devil is so close you feel his hot breath. He has to flee at the mention of the mighty name of Jesus! Roar your way to victory!

Chapter Nineteen
When the Dam is Broken

Indulge me for a few minutes as I give you some random facts and explain how these facts tie in with our daily lives. A dam is known as a barrier constructed to hold back water. Some dams are manmade, and some are made by creatures. Sometimes a dam is a necessity. For example, a dam is used to control water in a reservoir. Sometimes a dam is a nuisance. For example, when a beaver has stopped up the creek and causes the larger body of water to dry out. Have you ever heard someone say, "I'll be glad when the dam breaks?" They could be talking about an actual dam in the woods, or they could be metaphorically speaking about the junk in their life that causes them grief. How we fight in spiritual warfare is similar to a dam breaking… just bear with me.

There are five causes for a dam to break:

1. Overtopping
2. Defects in the Foundation
3. Cracks
4. Poor maintenance
5. Inadequate piping

Like a broken dam, the disconnects and struggles we deal with tend to happen because of negligence on our part. Don't you love it when you wake up with a song or scripture in your heart? Three days after my daughter was served the aforementioned papers, I woke up with this reminder from Psalm 23 "He will prepare a table for you in the presence of your enemies." Sometimes we don't understand the pain or process, but God is always working. He never sleeps. While we lay our heads down at night, He is working. When we get that in our hearts and truly believe it, we can enjoy so much peace. Am I saying I have it all together and have no stress? I am not saying that. I am saying I, too, have to remind myself of the goodness and faithfulness of God. He is for us. What we believe influences our being. Too often we focus on the problem or the enemy. We allow that focus to act as a Dam stopping up the flowing of our blessings or the strength of our faith. Are you aware there are multiple verses in the Bible that teach us about water and how it correlates to Jesus, our blessings, and our spirit man? Let's think about a few examples.

The first one that comes to mind is the story of the woman at the well. The Samaritan woman was desperately searching for something to make her feel satisfied or whole. She was a Samaritan, which meant she was in a lower class than the Jews. Women today deal with this same issue. Women are made to feel like they have to look a certain way, act a certain way, have a certain job, live in a certain neighborhood, cook elaborate meals, have a certain number of children who always look pristine, and numerous other things. Their self-worth is lost in the demands of society, which is absolutely brutal and unforgiving. Women are labeled and treated as if they are in a different class of people if they do not succumb to such fleshly demands. Just like the woman at the well, women today are in and out of relationships, have lost their stability, and have lost their purpose. Jesus asked the Samaritan woman for a drink, and she immediately told him she was a Samaritan, which was considered "less" than he. She explained that she shouldn't be allowed to offer him a drink since he was a Jew." Jesus responded, "If you knew the gift of God and who it is that asks you for a drink, you would have asked him and he would have given you living water…..Everyone who drinks this water will be thirsty again, but whoever drinks the water I give them will never thirst. Indeed, the water I give them will become in them a spring of water welling up to eternal life" (John 4). Jesus was saying who you are is more than a group, club, or societal standard. If you will call upon me and know my saving power, I can give you something that truly satisfies you and makes you whole. You can live with purpose and power. Women seek adoration, love, and affection because we were created as emotional beings. How can a woman fulfill the role of a nurturer or helpmate if she has zero emotions? (Side note, we also allow our emotions to get us in trouble and cause us pain when that was never the intention God had when He created us.)

Women are designed by God, and women are special to Him. The Samaritan woman was not saved. She didn't have the foundation necessary to empower her and provide her with confidence. The dam in her life was that she lacked a spiritual foundation, so she had no purpose or self-worth; she was unstable. Jesus offered her a solid foundation which would break every stronghold in her life. Secondly, Jesus referred to a spring of water welling up. One way a dam is broken is by water overtopping it. When Jesus fills you with His spirit, the water is flowing through you like a well springing forth, or like water overtopping the debris that has stopped up your blessings for long enough! That is why it is so important for us to constantly revive ourselves and keep His word flowing through us. He promises to keep our cups overflowing!

Another way a dam is broken is by cracking. This cause is very specific to me because it forces us to examine our lives daily. A crack in a dam is generally caused by the settling that takes place naturally. What about us? Do we get in a rut or routine that leaves us vulnerable? We do. On the other hand, can we force a dam to blow out (an obstacle or life issue) by being so persistent in prayer that we chip away at the stronghold little by little. One crack at a time will lead to pressure the devil can't handle. Keep pressing on and move that stuff out of your flow of goodness!

Consistent with cracks leading to a broken dam, the same is true if it is unkept or inadequately maintained. If the dam is meant to hold you back, and you continue to speak the word of God over your situation, the devil cannot man his station. That means the dam is left unprotected, unkept, or inadequately maintained. You keep speaking the promises of God and watch as the lies, deceit, and torment begin to crumble under the weight of the Living Water! Likewise, if we are the reason our spiritual life is bound up, we have to do a maintenance check. Are we praying? Are we reading the word? Are we saying one thing and acting like we believe another? We have to keep our spiritual armor in full working gear. We have to commit to the work.

The final issue that causes a dam to break is the poor filtration in the pipes. This could lead to an entire book alone, but I will be brief. If a dam's pipes take on seepage or debris, it will clog the pipes and lead to the other issues I've discussed. Do you need a breakthrough? Do you need the dam to break and the devil to pack his bags and go? Check your pipes. What's in your spirit? What are you watching? Eating? Drinking? Saying? Believing? Doing? The devil will look for a way to keep your pipes dirty. If he can make you do one thing today and another thing next week, he can slowly cause your pipes to have issues. When the Lord cleans you up, it is your choice to live cleanly. If you keep your pipes in check (we all have to), you will break the filth off of your life and the power and blessing of the Almighty will overtake you!

I don't know about you, but I am ready to break some dams off my life and off my family! God has called us to be like Him. He is alive and has given us the power to break these generational curses, addictions, bad habits, and societal strongholds. Go to war for your family. Check the issues in your life and see which of the five things mentioned are causing the devil to think he has won. He can't clog up the pathway of the plan God has for your life! Stand firm on your solid foundation and move off the devil's rickety playground.

Sandy Reid

Chapter Sixteen
Salt Water, Sun, Sand, and Reflections

Some things just make people happy. Different people like different environments, and my favorite environment is the beach. I have always loved everything about the sandy shores and salty seas.

I cannot count the number of hours I have spent wading in tide pools or searching for the perfect shell. Nonetheless, my love for such paradise has remained constant. One autumn, I decided to take a solo trip to the beach and just unwind and focus on feeding my spirit. The school district had a scheduled fall break in October, so I made my plans to stay at a resort for a couple of days. I wasn't sure how the weather would present itself, but I was certain I wouldn't let it stop me from dedicating time to draw closer to God. Life had become so busy, but I had allowed it. If there is one thing I know about a relationship with God it is that I cannot make it through life alone, and I have to be intentional about keeping myself close to Him. Trust me, sometimes I struggle with time. I can find more ways to stay busy than a colony of bees! Again, it is because time is a man-made constraint. It is my fault that I feel overwhelmed if I continue to say yes to every person or every demand put before me. I know this to be so, but I do it anyway. That is why it is important to steal away and regroup. Alone time can be transformational if we allow it and commit to it.

Once I settled in my room, I hurriedly made my way down to the sand-dusted pier which led to the beach. The sun was trading places with the moon, and the light from the transfer seemed to spotlight the rise and fall of the incoming tide. I listened to the frothy waves crash against the shore. I inhaled a deep breath laced with salt and felt a surge of excitement confirming I was where I needed to be. I walked a short distance before returning to my room for the night. I made sure I looked up the exact time the sun would rise the next morning. I wanted to be intentional about seeing the beauty of the sunrise and spending every moment I could enjoying my surroundings and learning whatever God wanted to teach me.

The following morning I woke up and probably jumped a little as I prepared to walk the beach. It was still dark outside, but the sunrise was promised. Very much like our lives sometimes- it is dark and uncertain. Sometimes we are upset because we have failed or we have allowed ourselves to be disappointed. Hang on! If we hold on to the promise, He says His mercies are new every day. Just like that sunrise that happens every single day -regardless of what else is going on- "His mercies are new for us every day." This encouraging reminder comes from the book of Lamentations. According to the Oxford Dictionary, Lamentations literally means "The passionate expression of grief or sorrow; weeping." So in the book about sorrow, God has promised to be steadfast with His love for us. He has promised us that no matter how dark the skies may turn, His love never ceases and His mercies are new every morning. If you are struggling with something today, consider the promise of a new sunrise tomorrow. Regardless of the circumstances, no matter how terrible the sin, He is faithful to deliver us and grant us unmerited favor. The key is to believe in the sunrise even when we can't see it. "For we walk by faith and not by sight" (2 Corinthians 5:7).

I woke up, got dressed, made my coffee, and rushed to get to the beach IN THE DARK because I believed I would see a sunrise. I never thought, "What if the sun doesn't rise today?" I just believed and knew the sun would rise. Are you feeling hopeless? Are you questioning if tomorrow will be any better? I encourage you to keep moving forward, even in the darkest of times. Believe there is a sunrise. The Light of the World will show up, I promise you.

Just as expected, at 6:50 AM the most spectacular sunrise peaked over the horizon. I stood watching and snapping pictures as the enormous light rose to its destination. I felt a sense of accomplishment and satisfaction. The sunlight was gorgeous as it showed off bright orange, red, and yellow hues. It was definitely worth waking up to see.

The second morning I had the same routine, but this time the dark skies were full of clouds, too. As I continued to walk down the shoreline and listen to the waves, I noticed several people had joined the wait. As the peak time drew nearer, the most intriguing situation happened. We all stood watching and waiting for the beauty of the sun to rise and shine forth. In our minds, we had already determined what it would look like. That is not at all what happened. Oddly enough, the clouds were surrounding the sun. I noticed the photographer looked through his lens several times but never took a shot. Within minutes, he put the lens cap back on his camera as he turned toward the path to the resort. He must have decided there was nothing worth capturing. Slowly, other people began to turn and walk toward the condos and hotels. I just stood there. I started to think about the situation and learned such a valuable lesson that morning. First, I realized that I could actually see the people and the details- like a photographer placing a lens cap on a camera or the lack of movement in his pointer finger proving he didn't take a photo. The ability to see those things was made possible by the light. Regardless of the clouds enveloping the sun, it was still there as promised. The sun was still giving off enough light to illuminate the world. Man, that was deep! I decided to take a seat on the sand and force my spirit man to listen intently for more truth. I watched the blurry ball float slowly to what seemed like the top of the world. I was reminded about how easy it is for things to get in our way as believers.

Oftentimes, it is the negative things that capture our attention. Sometimes it is the good things that distract us. As I mentioned before, we are a busy society. We allow ourselves to be overtaken by schedules, tasks, jobs, and pleasures. Am I saying we can't have good things in our lives? Absolutely not. I am saying we often allow things (good included) to block our view or detour our path? Indeed. Sometimes, when the obstacles come, we aren't patient enough to believe the light is still there. We are quick to shut down, turn away, or give up on a promise that is literally right before us. It took longer for the photographer to leave the beach than it did for the promise to take place. Even though the clouds were "in the way" of our view of the sun, the light was still there. The Lord says He will direct our steps. The psalmist wrote, "The Word is a lamp unto our feet and a light unto our path." If we are patient and wait on Him, the end result will be better than we imagined. He cares about the details! I waited on that sand, and as the sun rose higher in the sky, the clouds dissipated. During that process, the most beautiful arrays were extended toward the shore. I dare say if the photographer would have snapped a picture, that photo would have been even more beautiful than a photo of the previous day's sunrise. Psalm 37: 23-24 states,

The Lord directs the steps of the godly. He delights in every detail of their lives. Though they stumble, they will never fall, for the Lord holds them by the hand." Isn't that awesome? The Lord of heaven and earth delights in EVERY detail of your life! Why? Because He is merciful and He loves you so much. He only wants to provide new, beautiful things in your life- even in the midst of darkness and clouds. We must be patient and slow down so we can follow the light of direction.

Another favorite pastime of mine while at the beach is to look for shells. Since I was by myself, I had the freedom to walk as long and as far as I wanted. I definitely took advantage of that freedom. I combed the sands for each type of shell. I began to collect and place each one in my mesh bag. Like a child digging for treasure, I went from water to dunes in search of the perfect shells. I started talking to the Lord about searching for each one. I did this for hours every day. Each afternoon I would bring in my collection and wash them thoroughly. I had towels spread across the table and entertainment console so I could allow each shell to dry. My collection was so large, I had to purchase a basket just to bring them home. Talk about being proud! I was seriously ecstatic about my finds. I managed to find multiples of every type of shell on the "seashell hunt list." Some of the shells I found were huge, and some were dainty. Each one I discovered brought a smile to my face.

 The last day of my mini-vacay started just like the others. I was just talking to the Lord and said, "Now Lord, you have given me all these shells the past two days. The only thing I'm missing is a sand dollar." I combed the beach with my eyes and decided to walk up the sand just a bit. I saw a hodgepodge of broken shells and bent down to look at them. Suddenly, my eye spied two sand dollars! One teeny tiny one and one small one. I figured the tiny one was planted there for Maddie Lee & Callie. I was so excited.

 As I walked, I bent down to find another unique shell and noticed the tiny sand dollar was gone. I was so bummed but quickly said, " Lord it's ok. You gave me more than I asked for so I'm still grateful." Really, I was bummed though. I kept walking and looking at various shells. Just before I made it back to the pier I found another sandollar! I laughed and said, "Thanks Jesus, you are too good." I wondered if people on the beach were laughing at me since I was alone and laughing. Suddenly I heard a little voice, "Don't drink your coffee anymore. The tiny one is in the cup." I paused for a second and squinted my eyes with an, "Ok this is getting really good" look.

Anyone who knows me knows I love my coffee down to the last drop. So, to refrain from drinking any more of my morning brew was very intentional on my part. I got to my room and slowly poured out the remainder of my coffee. The creamy goodness began to spill out and make its way down the sink. I made sure the stopper was closed because unlike other times in my life when I doubted, I was ready to see this little supernatural splendor! The last bit of liquid pooled at the bottom of the sink. There wasn't a sand dollar in the hazelnut pool, but just as He promised, I found the tiny sand dollar at the bottom of the cup. I know this may sound absolutely ridiculous to many people, but for me it was reassurance of God's provision, humor, love, and attention to detail. He wants to give us the things that bring us joy, and he wants us to talk to him as his child- even if that means asking for a sand dollar. Everything we enjoy has been created by Him, and we can trust that He will provide for us.

Sandy Reid

Conclusion

As we have concluded the various chapters in this book, I urge you to take a moment to think about your own life and its chapters. Each chapter is not, nor has been, a surprise to our Lord. Rather, each is a part of God's ultimate plan. Take heart and know God is with you, and he has called our generation to do more than merely experience fear as we watch the creek rise. The tugging you've been feeling is His calling. He has called us to rise up and carry His truth throughout the world- that is His will. We have been waiting on someone to take the lead when really Jesus is our leader. All we have to do is surrender and commit to serving. WE are the army our family has taught us about over the years! WE are the ones equipped for battle. Just think, your wounds can be transformed into healing ointment for others in similar situations. Your testimony can be the sweet fragrance of hope and victory for a fellow neighbor. Your insecurities can be squelched by the overwhelming support from a blood-bought sisterhood/brotherhood in Christ. My friend, as the creek rises…We must take up the mantle. We are the ones chosen for such a time as this. May you be blessed as we join together to see His promises fulfilled and experience the greatest move of God ever!

In Christ,

Sandy

Sandy Reid

www.ingramcontent.com/pod-product-compliance
Lightning Source LLC
Chambersburg PA
CBHW041128110526
44592CB00020B/2731